Presented To:

_____

From:

_____

Date:

_____

❧

P.S. GOD LOVES YOU!

DEVOTIONAL

by Connie Witter

Honor Books
Tulsa, Oklahoma

P.S. God Loves You Devotional

ISBN1-56292-644-6

Copyright © 2001 by Connie Witter

Published by Honor Books

P.O. Box 55388

Tulsa, Oklahoma 74155

"For I know the plans I have for you,"
declares the LORD,
"plans to prosper you and not to harm you,
plans to give you hope and a future.
Then you will call upon me and come and pray to me,
and I will listen to you.
You will seek me and find me
when you seek me with all your heart.
I will be found by you," declares the LORD.

Jeremiah 29:11-14

Introduction

*I*n Philippians 3:10 AMP, the apostle Paul wrote of his desire to know God. He said, "[For my determined purpose is] that I may know Him [that I may progressively become more deeply and intimately acquainted with Him]." I believe that in the heart of every Christian lies this same desire to draw closer to God and come to know Him more fully.

God is a Person, and you can come to know Him the same way you came to know your spouse or your closest friend, by becoming intimately acquainted with Him through fellowship. God longs to have an intimate, loving relationship with you; this is the heart of the *P.S. God Loves You Devotional.* It was written so that you could come to know God's heart toward you as He speaks to you through His Word. As you respond to His words of love, you will come to know Him in a more real and personal way.

Taken strictly from Scripture and paraphrased into a love letter from God, each devotional will remind you of His unconditional love and His desire to see you live a successful and happy life. As you read each letter, you will hear Him saying again and again, "I love you;" "I have a wonderful plan for your life;" "Trust Me, I won't fail you."

It is my prayer that the *P.S. God Loves You Devotional* will draw you into a closer, more intimate love relationship with your Heavenly Father and with your Lord, Jesus Christ. Make sure to have your Bible with you during your devotional time, so that you can refer to the Scripture references. As you read each devotion and study the Scriptures, His promises will fill your heart with joy and peace!

Connie Witter

Contents

∾

God's Strength and Help

God's Blessings and Promises

God's Plan for Your Life

God's Strength

nd Help

Under the Shadow
of His Wings

᭼

I will lie down and sleep
in peace, for you alone,
O LORD, make me dwell in safety.
Psalm 4:8

*D*well in My presence by thinking upon My Word
and speaking the truth from your heart.

When you dwell in My secret place, you will abide under
the shadow of My wings. Say that I am your Refuge and your
Fortress—your God, in whom you confidently trust.

Then I promise to deliver you from the hand of the
enemy and from every deadly disease. I will cover you with
My feathers, and under My wings you will find refuge; My
truth and My faithfulness will shield you from all harm.

You have no reason to be afraid of the terror of the
night or the evil plots of the wicked that happen during
the day or the disease that stalks in darkness or the
destruction and sudden death that happen at noonday.

Although a thousand may fall at your side and ten
thousand at your right hand, it shall not come near you.

Because you have made Me your Refuge and your dwelling Place, no harm will befall you, nor will any plague or calamity come near your home. I will command My angels to take charge over you and protect you in all your ways.

Scripture Reading:

Psalm 15:1-2   Psalm 91:1-11

❧

Prayer:

Heavenly Father, when I'm tempted to be afraid, I will instead put my trust in You. You alone, Oh Lord, are my Refuge and Fortress. I look to You for safety and protection, for You are my God, and in You I confidently trust. I can trust You because You have promised to command Your angels to take charge over me and protect me from all harm. You are trustworthy, Lord, and I have absolutely no reason to be afraid, for You alone make me dwell in safety. In Jesus' name,   *Amen.*

God's Unfailing Love

❧

*The LORD appeared . . . saying: "I have
loved you with an everlasting love; I
have drawn you with loving-kindness."*
Jeremiah 31:3

I have drawn you to Me because of My great love
for you. You are so very precious to Me; My love
for you is unconditional. The truth is, there is absolutely
nothing you could do to cause Me to stop loving you.
Neither death nor life nor any power in all the world could
separate you from My great love. Nothing you've done in
the past or could do in the future would make Me withdraw
My love from you.

I want you to be established and secure in My love for
you, so you can grasp the breadth, length, height, and
depth of it. I want you to really come to know My love,
which far surpasses human knowledge, that you may be
filled with the fullness of Me.

Because of My great love for you, you can trust Me
completely, for I only want the very best for you. My plan

for your life is beyond what you could ever hope for or imagine. So rest secure in My unfailing love, knowing that I can bring to pass My purpose for your life—and do it superabundantly, far over and above your highest prayers, desires, thoughts, hopes, and dreams.

Scripture Reading:

Romans 8:38-39   Ephesians 3:17-21

❧

Prayer:

Heavenly Father, thank You for loving me unconditionally. No matter how many mistakes I make, You'll never stop loving me. I will rest secure in Your unfailing love, realizing that You only want the very best for me. I ask You to give me a deeper understanding of Your love, so that I might be filled with the fullness of You. I know You have a good plan for my life. I can trust You because I know You love me. You are able to bring to pass Your purpose for me and do exceedingly, abundantly above my highest hopes and dreams in every area of my life. In Jesus' name,   *Amen.*

Perfect Peace

❧

You will keep him in perfect peace,
him Whose mind is on You,
Because he trusts in You.
Isaiah 26:3 NKJV

I will keep you in perfect and constant peace when you keep your mind on Me and completely trust Me.

I have given you My peace. So don't let your heart be filled in any way with worry and fear.

Cast all your cares upon Me because I truly care about you. Don't worry about anything; instead, in every situation, simply pray and present your request to Me with a thankful heart. And My peace that passes all understanding will guard your heart and mind as you trust in Jesus.

I assure you that I will grant you whatever you ask in the name of My Son, Jesus. So ask and you will receive, and your joy will be full. I have promised you this so that in Me you may have perfect peace and confidence in the midst of any problem you may face.

Finally, My child, fix your thoughts on what is true, good, and right. Think about things that are pure and lovely, and dwell on the good things in others. Think about everything for which you can praise Me, and My peace will always be with you.

Scripture Reading:

John 14:27	1 Peter 5:7
John 16:23-24,33	Philippians 4:6-9

❧

Prayer:

Heavenly Father, I know that when I worry, it's because I'm not truly trusting You. Please forgive me and help me trust You more by keeping my mind on You and Your wonderful promises. Remind me to focus on those things that are lovely and of a good report and to dwell on the good things in my spouse, children, and others. I will meditate and think upon all that I can praise You for. Thank You for Your promise to answer my prayers. I know that as I trust You completely, I will have Your perfect peace. In Jesus' name, Amen.

God Knows You Intimately

❧

*How precious it is, Lord, to realize
that you are thinking about me
constantly! I can't even count
how many times a day your
thoughts turn towards me.*
Psalm 139:17 TLB

*M*y child, I know everything about you—your heart's deepest thoughts, feelings, and desires. Before you speak a word, I know what you'll say. I notice everything you do and everywhere you are. There's no place you can go that My presence doesn't follow, for I'm always watching over you.

A hair cannot fall from your head without My notice. I know you so intimately that each one is numbered.

Long ago, before you were ever conceived, I knew you. I created you in your mother's womb and watched in secret as your body was formed. I wrote My plan for you in My book before you took your first breath.

Never *for one minute* think you were a mistake. For in truth, you've been part of My plan from the beginning of time. I created you to be alive—now—at this exact moment.

There is no one in all the world just like you. You were fearfully and wonderfully hand-crafted by Me. Do you realize that I think about you constantly? My thoughts turn toward you countless times each day. I want you to understand just how precious and valuable you are to Me.

Scripture Reading:

Psalm 139:1-18   Matthew 10:29-31
Jeremiah 1:5   Esther 4:14

⌒❧

Prayer:

Heavenly Father, You know everything about me. Even before I was conceived, You wrote Your plan for me. I was already in Your heart and mind. It's hard to comprehend that even though there are millions of people in the world, You still think about me constantly. Although that seems impossible, I choose to believe it because it's written in Your Word. Thank You for caring so tenderly for me and watching over me so closely. I know You have a good plan for my life, and I ask for Your wisdom and guidance that I might fulfill the purpose for which You created me. In Jesus' name,   *Amen.*

Fear Not!

～

For I am the LORD, your God, who takes
hold of your right hand and says to you,
Do not fear; I will help you.
Isaiah 41:13

*D*on't be afraid, for I have ransomed you; I have
called you by name; you are mine. When you go
through deep waters and great trouble, I will be with you.
When you go through rivers of difficulty, you will not
drown! When you walk through the fire of oppression, you
will not be burned up—the flames will not consume you.
For I am the Lord your God, your Savior.

Fear not, (there is nothing to fear) for I am with you;
do not look around you in terror and be dismayed, for I am
your God. I will strengthen and harden you (to difficulties);
yes, I will help you; yes, I will hold you up and retain you
with My victorious right hand.

I will not in any way fail you nor give you up nor leave
you without support. I will not! I will not in any degree

leave you helpless nor forsake nor let you down!
Assuredly Not!

Scripture Reading:

Isaiah 43:1-3   Isaiah 41:10

Hebrews 13:5

⤚

Prayer:

*Heavenly Father, I will not fear when I go through
difficulties, for You have promised to help me and uphold
me with Your victorious right hand. If You are on my side,
who can succeed at coming against me? Lord, I put my
trust in You, for I know that You will not fail to bring me
victory in every situation. In Jesus' name,*   *Amen.*

The Testing of Your Faith

These trials are only to test your faith, to see whether or not it is strong and pure. It is being tested as fire tests gold and purifies it—and your faith is far more precious to God than mere gold; so if your faith remains strong after being tried in the test tube of fiery trials, it will bring you much praise and glory and honor on the day of his return.
1 Peter 1:7 TLB

*B*e joyful, My child, whenever you encounter trials in your life. Don't be discouraged. Be assured and understand that the trying of your faith develops steadfastness and patience in you. Let patience fully develop in you; then you will come through your trial, strong in character, not lacking any good thing.

These trials have come to test your faith, to see if it is strong and pure. Don't make the mistake of believing that these trials come from Me; you have an enemy that wants to steal your faith in My Word. Be aware of his plan.

As you come to trust the promises of My Word, don't be surprised if the enemy immediately urges you to give up. The situation may seem to worsen before it improves, but be sure not to abandon your steadfast confidence in Me. Continue to trust Me with patience, and I will reward your faith. If you do not give up, you will fully accomplish My will in your life; then you will receive and enjoy to the fullest all that I have promised you.

Scripture Reading:

Luke 8:11-15　　　　　James 1:2-4, 12-13

Hebrews 10:35-36

❧

Prayer:

Heavenly Father, give me the strength to stand strong on Your Word when I face trials that test my faith. I will remember that the enemy comes to steal Your Word from me, but by Your grace I won't give up. I will be patient and put my confidence in Your promise of victory. I'll rejoice in Your Word in the midst of my trials, for I know my prayers will be answered and Your promises will come to pass in my life. In Jesus' name,　　　　　Amen.

The Father's Love

~&

*The Lord your God is in the midst
of you, a Mighty One, a Savior
[Who saves]! He will rejoice over
you with joy; He will rest [in silent
satisfaction] and in His love He
will be silent and make no mention
[of past sins, or even recall them];
He will exult over you with singing.*
Zephaniah 3:17 AMP

Long ago, before I created the world, I chose you
to be My child, through Jesus' sacrifice for you.
Though you may think you chose Me, the truth is that *I
chose you first!* Through your faith in Jesus, I've made you
holy in My eyes—without a single fault—and covered you
with My love.

To satisfy My love for you, even when you were
spiritually dead from your sins, I made you alive through
My Son, Jesus. You were saved by My grace.

When I sent My Son to be punished for your sins so
you could partake of My blessings, I proved then how very
much I love you. So never doubt My love for you;
remember, long before you ever loved Me, I loved you first!

You're My child, and I delight in you. Don't recall your past mistakes, for in My love they are forgiven and forgotten. Because of your faith in Jesus, you stand pure and holy in My sight, and I rejoice over you with singing!

Scripture Reading:

Ephesians 1:3-6	*John 15:16*
Ephesians 2:4-5	*1 John 4:9-10*

Prayer:

Heavenly Father, thank You for choosing me as Your child. I know how You must love me to be willing to sacrifice Your only Son, so I could partake in Your promised blessings. I will rest in Your love, for I know You delight in me. Through Jesus, You have made me pure and holy in Your sight, and You rejoice over me with singing. I won't dwell on my past mistakes because I know You have forgiven me, and they are completely forgotten. I love You, Lord, because I realize just how much You first loved me. In Jesus' name,   *Amen.*

God's Forgiveness

*If we confess our sins, he is faithful
and just and will forgive us our sins
and purify us from all unrighteousness.*
1 John 1:9

*M*y child, when you confess your sins to Me and
ask for forgiveness, I'm always faithful to
forgive you and cleanse you from all unrighteousness.

I won't hold your sins against you. Not only will I
forgive your sins, but I will also completely and
permanently forget them.

I made you, and I will not forget to help you. I've
blotted out your sins; they are gone like the morning mist
at noon! Oh, return to Me, for I have already paid the price
to set you free.

Don't let guilt rob you of your peace and joy. Forget
the former things; do not dwell on the past. I—even I—am
He who blots out your transgressions and remembers your
sins no more.

When you trust in Jesus to forgive your sins, you stand
pure and holy before Me without a single fault. You are

righteous in My sight, and I take great delight in you. I rejoice over you with singing.

Scripture Reading:

Hebrews 8:12	Isaiah 44:21-22
Isaiah 43:18,25	Ephesians 1:3-7
Acts 13:38-39	Zephaniah 3:17

❧

Prayer:

Heavenly Father, I ask You to forgive me for anything I have done that has not been pleasing to You. I ask You to cleanse me from all unrighteousness. I thank You for Your promise not only to forgive, but also to completely forget my sins. I am cleansed through the blood of Jesus, and I stand pure and holy in Your eyes because of Him. In Jesus' name,   *Amen.*

Divine Guidance

*This is what the LORD says—your
Redeemer, the Holy One of Israel:
"I am the LORD your God, who teaches
you what is best for you, who directs
you in the way you should go."*
Isaiah 48:17

*D*on't worry and fret over decisions you need to
make; simply ask Me to guide you down the right
path. As you look to Me and begin to trust and thank Me
for guiding you, My peace that passes all understanding
will keep your mind and heart at rest.

Put your confidence in Me, knowing that your every
step is directed by Me. I'm actively involved in your life,
pointing you toward true success. You may already have
many plans in your mind, but it is My purpose for you that
will prevail in the end.

Trust Me with all your heart, and don't lean to your
own understanding. Don't try to figure out everything on
your own; this will only lead to confusion. Instead, when
you have a decision to make, acknowledge Me by inquiring
what to do. I will guide you by turning your heart and mind
in the direction of My will.

So don't fear making the wrong choice; instead, keep your mind on Me and begin thanking Me for directing and guiding you. I'll make sure you go down the correct path, and you'll never have to fear being out of My will.

Scripture Reading:

Psalm 37:23   Philippians 4:6-7
Proverbs 19:21   Proverbs 3:5-6

❧

Prayer:

Heavenly Father, I ask for Your guidance and direction in my life. I ask You to turn my heart and mind in the direction of Your will. I'm trusting You to guide me in the way I should go. I won't worry about the decisions I need to make. Instead, I'll keep my mind on You and the wonderful promises You have given me. I'll acknowledge You, Lord, in every decision that I make. Thank You for guiding and directing me toward Your perfect plan for my life. In Jesus' name,   Amen.

God's Purpose for You

*I will cry to God Most High, Who
performs on my behalf and rewards me
[Who brings to pass His purposes for
me and surely completes them]!*
Psalm 57:2 AMP

I'm your Heavenly Father, and I know the purpose
I have for your life. I created you for a special
reason. I have prepared a specific plan just for you. It's
never too late to begin resting in My unfailing love and
trusting your life to Me. Then I can work on your behalf,
fulfilling My purpose and making you into everything I
created you to be.

You are My masterpiece. I created you to accomplish
great things upon the earth. Everything I have for you to
do, I planned before the world was ever created.

I have given you gifts and talents that will never be
taken from you. It's My desire that you would use them for
My glory.

So look to Me, My child. Begin to pray for My will and
purpose to be accomplished in your life. Simply trust Me to

bring to pass My plan for you; then I will perform on your behalf and reward you. Yes, I will bring to pass My purpose for you and surely complete it!

Scripture Reading:

Philippians 1:6	*Psalm 139:13, 16*
Ephesians 2:10	*Romans 11:29*

❧

Prayer:

Heavenly Father, I trust my life to You. I know You have a wonderful plan for me. I ask You to bring to pass Your specific plan in my life. I'm trusting You to perform on my behalf and reward me, to bring to pass Your purposes for me and surely complete them! Thank You for working in me and changing me into everything You created me to be. I know Your purpose for me will be accomplished because You are faithful to Your promises. In Jesus' name. Amen.

A God-given Vision

For the vision is yet for the appointed time; It hastens toward the goal, and it will not fail. Though it tarries, wait for it; For it will certainly come, it will not delay.
Habakkuk 2:3 NAS

*A*s your Heavenly Father, I have placed dreams and visions in your heart—the things you desire to do in your life—as part of My plan for you. Write them down, so you may think on them and put them into action.

Your vision is for a specific time. Don't despair if it seems slow in coming; just be patient and continue to believe. Never let go of your vision nor doubt for one moment that it will materialize. I promise to bring it to pass in My perfect timing; simply do your part and trust Me completely—and watch as I do the rest!

Now you are in a training period, preparing for what lies ahead. So turn from evil and pursue righteousness. Seek to be more like Jesus in your thoughts, words, and actions. Trust Me to work in you. Then you'll be My vessel of honor, ready to do the work I have for you.

Before you know it—at the precise time—I will open doors for you that no man will be able to close. I will use you in a mighty way to bring to pass My will upon the earth.

Scripture Reading:

Habakkuk 2:2-4   2 Timothy 2:21-22

Revelations 3:7-8

❧

Prayer:

Heavenly Father, I won't let go of the vision that You have placed within me. These dreams and desires are part of Your plan for my life. I will write Your plan down, so I can read it and run with it. I want to use the gifts You have given me to accomplish Your will on this earth. I'm trusting You to work in me by the power of Your Spirit, that my character might reflect the character of Jesus. Then I'll be ready to do the work You have for me. I'm trusting You, Lord, to bring to pass Your perfect plan for me. In Jesus' name,   *Amen.*

God Will Take Care of You

He tends his flock like a shepherd:
He gathers the lambs in his arms
and carries them close to his heart.
Isaiah 40:11

*A*s a good shepherd provides for his sheep, I will provide for you. Rest peacefully and be secure in My loving arms, for I hold you ever so close to My heart because you are so special and valuable to Me.

I have created you, and I will care for you. I'm your Heavenly Father, and I made you and have cared for you throughout your whole life. I have never forsaken you.

When you cry for help in the time of trouble, I always hear you and come to deliver you from all your fears. My angels encamp around you and deliver you from all your troubles.

Look to Me as your Provider, as a sheep does a shepherd, and you will not lack any good thing. Yes, I will take care of you. I will open My hand and provide for you. Others around you may lack the necessities of life, but you will have all that you need. You will taste and see My goodness; you will be blessed, happy, and fortunate because you put your complete trust in Me.

Scripture Reading:

Psalm 23:1   Psalm 145:16

Isaiah 46:3-4   Psalm 34:6-10

~

Prayer:

Heavenly Father, I can rest peacefully in Your loving arms, knowing that You will take care of me. There's no need to worry or fear; You hold me tenderly close to Your heart. You give me great peace. I put my trust in You, knowing that You will provide for my every need. I know I will continue to see Your goodness in my life. In Jesus' name,   Amen.

Cast Your Cares upon the Lord

❧

Casting the whole of your care [all your anxieties, all your worries, all your concerns, once and for all] on Him, for He cares for you affectionately and cares about you watchfully.
1 Peter 5:7 AMP

*C*ast all your cares and concerns on Me, for I tenderly watch over you and care for you affectionately.

Cast down every worried and anxious thought and begin thinking upon My promises to you, for I will keep you in perfect and constant peace when you keep your mind on Me.

There has never been another god like Me; I truly care about you and everything you are going through. I see your situation; I know your heart's desire, and I'm willing to move powerfully on your behalf. All that I ask of you is to put your complete trust in Me.

Don't worry about anything. Instead, pray about the situation and then trust Me to take care of it for you. Begin to thank Me for working on your behalf. I'm your Heavenly

Father, and I have promised to perfect everything that
concerns you.

Scripture Reading:

2 Corinthians 10:5   *Isaiah 64:4*

Philippians 4:6-7   *Isaiah 26:3-4*

Psalm 138:8

⌐❧

Prayer:

*Heavenly Father, I give You my worries and concerns,
and I replace them with thoughts of Your promises. I
rejoice in what You have promised me, for when I put my
trust in You, You will bring to pass the desires of my
heart. I have no need to worry about any situation
because You are willing and able to take care of everything
that concerns me. In Jesus' name,*   *Amen.*

God Will Never Forsake You

Never will I leave you;
never will I forsake you.
Hebrews 13:5

A woman may forget her nursing child, or she may even desert the baby who was born from her womb—yet I will never forget you. You are My beloved child, and I have imprinted your picture on the palm of each of My hands.

I am with you, and I will never leave you. I'm watching over you with care wherever you go. I will be a Father to you, for you are My child.

I have created you and cared for you
since you were born.
I will be your God through all your lifetime,
yes, even when your hair is white with age.
I made you and I will care for you.
I will carry you along and be your Savior.

Isaiah 46:3-4 TLB

Be strong and courageous. Don't be afraid or terrified, for I am with you. I will be your Refuge and Stronghold in the time of trouble. You can trust Me because I will never fail you nor forsake you.

Rest assured that nothing will ever separate you from My love, for surely I will be with you always, even to the very end of the world.

Scripture Reading:

Isaiah 49:15-16   Genesis 28:15

2 Corinthians 6:18   Deuteronomy 31:6

Psalm 62:8   Romans 8:36

Matthew 28:20

❧

Prayer:

Heavenly Father, how comforting it is to know that no matter what I go through, You are always right beside me, watching over me and caring for me so tenderly! Though others may forget about me and let me down, You will never forget about me because my picture is imprinted in the palms of Your hands. I can be confident and secure knowing that You will never leave me nor fail me. Nothing can ever separate me from Your great love. In Jesus' name,   Amen.

God is Faithful

God is faithful (reliable, trustworthy, and therefore ever true to His promise, and He can be depended on).
1 Corinthians 1:9 AMP

I am faithful and true to My promises, and you can completely depend on Me; I'm not a man that I should lie, nor do I change My mind. Do I speak and then not act? Do I promise and not fulfill?

Because I wanted to convince you that My plan and purpose for your life would never change, I confirmed My promises with an oath. I did this so that when you grab hold of the hope I have offered you in My Word, you will be greatly encouraged because it is impossible for Me to lie.

Hold fast, without wavering, to the hope you confess, for I am faithful to My Word. I will never stop loving you nor let My promises fail. I will not break My covenant nor change what I have said, for I am watching over My Word to make sure it comes to pass.

I am your Lord; when you put your hope in Me, you will never be disappointed. Not one of all the wonderful promises that I have given you will fail because My love for you is higher than the heavens, and My faithfulness reaches to the skies.

Scripture Reading:

1 Corinthians 1:9	*Numbers 23:19*
Hebrews 6:17-18	*Hebrews 10:23*
Psalm 89:33-34	*Jeremiah 1:12*
Isaiah 49:23	*Joshua 23:14*
Psalm 108:5	

~&

Prayer:

Heavenly Father, because You are so faithful, I can completely and confidently put my trust in all of Your promises. Because You have confirmed Your promises to me with an oath, I can be absolutely sure that You will perform them in my life. I cling to the hope You have offered me in Your Word and am greatly encouraged because I know it is impossible for You to lie. Not one of all the wonderful promises You have given me will fall short, for Your unfailing love abounds toward me, and Your faithfulness reaches to the skies. In Jesus' name,

Amen.

A Heart of Worship

Worship the LORD with gladness; come
before him with joyful songs.
Psalm 100:2

*W*orship Me with a glad heart; come before Me
with joyful songs. Know that I am God. I made
you, and you are Mine. I have chosen you to be My own.
You are My treasured possession.

Worship Me with all of your heart. Worship Me in spirit
and in truth; these are the kind of worshipers I seek.

Rejoice as you take refuge in Me; sing and shout for joy
because I make a covering over you and defend you. Surely
I will bless you and surround you with favor, as a shield.

Worship Me, the Lord your God, for it is I who delivers
you from the hand of the enemy.

You have set your love upon Me; therefore I will deliver
you. I will set you on high because you trust and rely upon
Me, knowing that I will never fail you—no, never.

When you call upon Me in times of trouble, I will answer you. I will deliver you and honor you. I will bless you with a long, good life and show you My salvation.

Scripture Reading:

Psalm 100:2-3   Psalm 135:4

John 4:23-24   Psalm 5:11-12

2 Kings 17:39   Psalm 91:14-16

Prayer:

Heavenly Father, I worship You with all my heart, for You are so loving and good. I'm Your treasured possession, and I know that You love me with all of Your heart. I love You, Heavenly Father, with all that is within me. You deliver me from the hand of the enemy. As I put my trust in You, I know You will never fail me. When I call upon You in times of trouble, You will answer me. You will deliver and honor me. With long life You will satisfy me and show me Your salvation. I will love and worship You all the days of my life. In Jesus' name,   *Amen.*

God Will Strengthen You

~

*The LORD gives strength to
his people; the LORD blesses
his people with peace.*
Psalm 29:11

I am your Lord, the Creator of the whole world; I never faint nor become weary.

Look to Me and My strength; seek to be in My presence continually. Rejoice in Me and be glad, My beloved; sing with an upright heart. Surely I am your Salvation. Trust in Me and do not be afraid, for I am your Strength and your Song.

I will give you power when you are weary and discouraged. When you feel weak, I will increase your strength, causing it to multiply and making it abound.

Even youths shall faint and become weary, and young men shall stumble and fall, exhausted, but when you look to Me with a confident expectation, I will renew your strength. You will soar on wings as eagles; you will run and not be weary; you will walk and not faint or become tired.

I am your God. I will strengthen and harden you to difficulties. Yes, I will help you; yes, I will hold you up and retain you with My victorious right hand.

Scripture Reading:

Isaiah 40:28-31   *1 Chronicles 16:11*
Psalm 32:11   *Isaiah 12:2*
Isaiah 41:10

❧

Prayer:

Heavenly Father, when I am weary and discouraged, I will look to You, for You are my Strength and my Song. Fill me with Your strength so that I might soar as an eagle. Then I will run with purpose and not be weary. I will walk and not faint. When I feel weak, I will look to You and Your promise. I know that You will strengthen me in times of difficulty, and by Your grace You will make me strong. In Jesus' name,   *Amen.*

The Lord is Your Shepherd

❧

The Lord is Shepherd [to feed, guide, and shield me], I shall not lack.
Psalm 23:1 AMP

I am your Shepherd. I will feed you, guide you, and protect you all the days of your life. You shall not lack in any way.

You are My sheep, the sheep of My pasture, and I am your God. I made you, and you are Mine. As a shepherd looks after his scattered flock when he is with them, so will I look after you. I will be your Shepherd and cause you to lie down in peace.

I will make you to lie down in green pastures; I will lead you beside still waters. I will refresh and restore your soul; I will lead you in paths of righteousness, not because you've earned it, but for My name's sake.

Though you may walk through the valley of the shadow of death, fear no evil, for I am with you; My rod will protect you; My staff will guide you and bring you comfort.

I prepare a table before you in the presence of your enemies. I anoint your head with oil; your cup overflows with My blessings.

Surely My goodness and love will follow you all the days of your life, and you will dwell in My house forever.

Scripture Reading:

Psalm 23:1-6   Ezekiel 34:12,15,31

Psalm 100:3

❧

Prayer:

Heavenly Father, You are my Shepherd. You provide for me, guide me, and protect me every day of my life. I shall not lack in any area of my life. You make me lie down in peace; You restore and revive my soul. You lead me in paths of righteousness, not because I earned it, but for Your name's sake. Though I walk through difficult times, I will not fear because You are with me, guiding and comforting me. Surely Your goodness and mercy will follow me all the days of my life, and I will dwell in Your house forever. In Jesus' name,   *Amen.*

Overcoming Temptation

*No temptation has seized you
except what is common to man.
And God is faithful; he will not let
you be tempted beyond what you
can bear. But when you are tempted,
he will also provide a way out so
that you can stand up under it.*
1 Corinthians 10:13

The temptations in your life are nothing new and different. Many others face these same trials. But I promise you won't be tempted and tried beyond your ability to overcome. I will provide a way, so you can stand strong against these trials and temptations.

When you're tempted, don't say, "God is doing it," for I can't be tempted by evil, nor do I tempt anyone. Only good and perfect things come from My hand, and that will never change.

However, your enemy, the devil, brings temptations and trials into your life. So watch and pray that you do not fall into temptation. Although your spirit is willing, your body is weak.

My Son, Jesus, was tempted just as you are at times, yet He did not sin. So come boldly to Me when you are tempted and I will grant mercy for your failures. I will strengthen you by My grace. You are My beloved child, and I will always help you in your time of need.

Scripture Reading:

1 Corinthians 10:13	James 1:13-17
1 Peter 5:8	Matthew 4:1
Matthew 26:41	Hebrews 4:15-16

Prayer:

Heavenly Father, it is comforting to know You will never let me be tempted without providing a way of escape. You promised me victory in every test and trial. I realize You do not bring these things into my life, for only good and perfect things come from Your hand. Therefore, I will watch carefully so the devil does not catch me off guard. I will fill my spirit with Your Word, so I become strong in You. I confidently ask to receive Your mercy and grace in my life. Thank You, Father, for helping me overcome victoriously in every temptation and trial. I love You, Lord, for You are so good to me. In Jesus' name, Amen.

God Will Comfort You

As a mother comforts her child,
so will I comfort you.
Isaiah 66:13

J am your Heavenly Father, who showers you with
My love and mercy. My heart is filled with
compassion toward you. I comfort you in all your troubles,
enabling you to comfort and encourage others who are
going through trouble and distress in the same manner.

As a mother comforts her child when he or she is afraid
or hurting, I will comfort you. Though you may be hurting
and distressed right now, joy will come in the morning.

I have seen you tossing and turning through the night.
I have collected all your tears and preserved them in My
bottle. I have recorded every one in My book. I hear your
cries, and I will comfort you and deliver you from distress.

I will turn your mourning into gladness; I will give you
comfort and joy instead of sorrow. I will mend your broken
heart and bind up your wounds, healing your pain. I will
bestow on you beauty instead of ashes, joy instead of
mourning, praise instead of a spirit of heaviness.

As you arise from the depression that these circumstances have kept you in, you will rise to a new life. You will shine and be radiant with My love and compassion; because I will pour My Spirit upon you, and My glory shall be seen on you.

Scripture Reading:

Psalm 103:2,4	*2 Corinthians 1:3-4*
Isaiah 66:13	*Psalm 30:5*
Psalm 56:8-13	*Psalm 34:17*
Jeremiah 31:13	*Psalm 147:3*
Isaiah 60:1-2	*Isaiah 61:1-3*

❧

Prayer:

Heavenly Father, You see my every tear. You know that my heart is hurting and You hear my every cry. You have seen me tossing and turning in the night and have put my tears in Your bottle and written them in Your book. Comfort me, Lord, with Your love and compassion. I will rest in Your loving arms, knowing that You are healing and restoring me. I will arise from this situation and shine with Your glory, for Your love for me never fails. In Jesus' name,   *Amen.*

God's Throne of Grace

❧

*Let us then approach the throne of
grace with confidence, so that we
may receive mercy and find grace
to help us in our time of need.*
Hebrews 4:16

*M*y beloved child, I desire to have fellowship
with you. So come before My throne of grace
with confidence, for I will always be merciful and gracious
toward you.

You never have to run from Me when you've done
wrong. I'm not angry with you. I will always love you no
matter what you do.

Through your faith in Jesus you may approach Me
with freedom and confidence.

When you trust in Jesus for the forgiveness of your
sins, you are holy in My sight without a single fault; you
stand before Me covered with My love. Jesus presents you
sinless and perfect before My glorious presence, and I
rejoice over you with ecstatic delight.

Therefore, since you have confidence to approach My
throne of grace by the blood of Jesus, draw near to Me
with a sincere heart in full assurance of faith and be
cleansed from a guilty conscience.

When you draw near to Me, I will draw near to you. I will make known to you the paths of life and fill you with joy in My presence.

Scripture Reading:

1 John 1:3	Hebrews 4:16
Isaiah 54:9-10	Ephesians 3:12
Ephesians 1:4-5	Jude 1:24
Zephaniah 3:17	Hebrews 10:19-23
James 4:8	Acts 2:28

Prayer:

Heavenly Father, forgive me for my failures and cleanse me from a guilty conscience. I know I shouldn't run from You when I do things that are wrong. You are a caring and forgiving Father who loves me unconditionally. I can approach Your throne of grace with confidence because Jesus presents me, faultless and perfect in Your glorious presence. Show me the paths of life, Lord. I want to be in fellowship with You, for You will fill me with joy in Your presence. In Jesus' name,   *Amen.*

God's Protection

Jehovah himself is caring for you!
He is your defender. He protects
you day and night. He keeps you
from all evil, and preserves your life.
He keeps his eye upon you as you
come and go, and always guards you.
Psalm 121:5-8 TLB

J am your Heavenly Father, and I will take care of you. I will protect you day and night. I will keep My eyes upon you wherever you go and be your Defender.

My name is a strong tower; when you run to it, you will be safe.

When you put your trust in Me, you'll be as secure as a mountain; no matter what comes against you, you won't be moved. Just as the mountains surround and protect Jerusalem, so I, the Lord, will surround and protect you.

Follow My wisdom, and it will bring you life. Then you will walk securely, and your feet will not stumble off My path. As you lie down to rest, you will have sweet, peaceful sleep.

P. S. GOD LOVES YOU!

So don't be afraid of sudden disaster, for I will be your confidence, firm and strong; I will keep you from hidden danger.

My angels will encamp around you and deliver you. Oh, taste and see that I am good! You are blessed because you trust and take refuge in Me.

Scripture Reading:

Psalm 121:5-8	*Proverbs 18:10*
Psalm 125:1-2	*Proverbs 3:21-26*
Psalm 34:7-8	

Prayer:

Heavenly Father, I ask You to protect me. I will rest in Your love and faithfulness. I choose to believe Your Word. You have promised to watch over and protect me wherever I go and to keep me safe from harm. I have no reason to be afraid, for You are my Refuge and my Stronghold. You will protect me from all danger when I put my trust in You. In Jesus' name,   Amen.

Victory over Trials

I am God, your God. . . . call on Me
in the day of trouble; I will deliver you,
and you shall honor and glorify Me.
Psalm 50:7,15 AMP

*T*here is not one trial that you have faced that others have not also experienced. I am faithful, and I won't allow you to be tried beyond your ability and power to overcome. In every trial, I will provide a way of escape, so you might enjoy victory.

Though trials and troubles may seem to surround you, and they may be pressing on you at every side, I will bring you safely through them. So look to Me with confidence, for I know how to deliver you out of all your trials.

Individuals of the Bible such as Abraham, David, Ruth, King Jehosophat, Esther, Moses, and Paul chose to worship Me in the midst of their trials, and I brought them through in victory. So offer up to Me a sacrifice of praise, My child, and I will also lead *you* to victory.

Yes, as you put your complete trust in Me and begin to thank Me for the victory, I will move on your behalf, and you will stand and see the salvation of the Lord.

Scripture Reading:

1 Corinthians 10:13	*Psalm 138:7-8*
2 Peter 2:9	*2 Chronicles 16:9*
Psalm 50:23	*2 Chronicles 20:1-22*

Prayer:

Heavenly Father, I will worship and praise You for the victory in the midst of every trial I face. For You have promised in Your Word to deliver me out of them all. Therefore, I will look to You with confidence and rejoice in Your promise. Please give me the grace I need to stand strong on Your Word and lift my voice in praise until I see Your salvation. In Jesus' name,   *Amen.*

Don't Be Discouraged

❧

O my soul, don't be discouraged.
Don't be upset. Expect God to act! For
I know that I shall again have plenty
of reason to praise him for all that he
will do. He is my help! He is my God!
Psalm 42:11 TLB

$\mathcal{M}$y child, don't be discouraged. Put your hope in Me! You become discouraged because you look at your circumstances instead of My promises, or you focus on others and believe that they have the power to keep My plan from working in your life.

That's not true. My Word says that I will work on your behalf. What man can hinder or prevent it? Is any man more powerful than I? I have the power to change the heart of a king.

I long to fill your life with My blessings, but in order for Me to do that, you must keep your eyes focused on Me; you must believe My Word. Don't allow your circumstances to discourage you. Believe the truth of My Word instead of the lies of the enemy.

Look to Me and fill your mind and heart with My promises. Then you'll be filled with joy and peace, overflowing with hope by the power of My Spirit.

Don't be discouraged or upset. Expect Me to act on your behalf, and you shall have plenty of reasons for which to praise Me. I am your help! I am your God!

Scripture Reading:

Psalm 42:11	*Isaiah 43:13*
Proverbs 21:1	*Isaiah 30:18*
James 1:6-7	*Hebrews 12:2*
Romans 15:13	*Psalm 43:5*

❦

Prayer:

Heavenly Father, I know that when I'm discouraged it's because I'm looking at something other than You. Please forgive me for believing the lies of the enemy over the truth of Your Word. I choose to fill my heart and mind with Your promises and believe that You will bring them to pass in my life. As I delight myself in You, my heart will be filled with joy, and my life will overflow with Your blessings. In Jesus' name,   *Amen.*

God's Grace is Sufficient

❧

The grace of God (the unmerited favor and merciful kindness by which God, exerting His holy influence upon souls, turns them to Christ, and keeps, strengthens, and increases them in Christian virtues).
2 Corinthians 1:12 AMP

*W*hen you try to obey My Word in your own strength, you become discouraged because in your own ability you can do nothing.

I want you to trust Me and rely on My power to work within you. Many times you try to do things in your own strength and ability. Yet My Spirit yearns within you, waiting for an invitation—waiting for you to ask for My help. Ask Me to strengthen and change you, for My grace is available if you are only humble enough to receive it.

As you rely upon Me, My grace will be at work in your life. I will exert My holy influence upon your mind, your will, and your emotions. I will strengthen you by My Spirit and make you increase in Christian character.

When you feel weak, My grace will strengthen you. My power is most effective when it turns your weaknesses into

My strengths. For when you are weak in yourself, My grace will make you strong! So come boldly to My throne of grace. Ask, and I will give you mercy and forgiveness for your failures and the grace to strengthen you into everything I have called you to be.

Scripture Reading:

John 15:5	*Philippians 4:13*
James 4:5-6	*2 Corinthians 1:12 AMP*
2 Corinthians 12:9-10	*Hebrews 4:15-16*

❧

Prayer:

Heavenly Father, I come boldly to Your throne of grace and ask You to strengthen and change me into everything You want me to be. Forgive me for depending on myself and my own ability to be good. I want to instead rely and trust in You to work in me. For I know Your grace is sufficient for my every weakness. Please let the power of Your grace effectively work in me, changing me into Your image, so I become more like You. In Jesus' name,

Amen.

Changed by His Grace

*Much more surely will those who
receive [God's] overflowing grace
(unmerited favor) and the free gift of
righteousness . . . reign as kings in life
through the one Man Jesus Christ.*
Romans 5:17 AMP

I want you to daily receive My overflowing grace
in your life by humbly asking Me to help you to
walk in My Word; only then will you bear the fruit of
righteousness and reign victorious in this life.

As you daily trust Me to strengthen you, My grace will
be poured out upon your life. I will strengthen you and
make you what you ought to be. I will equip you with
everything you need to do My will. Yes, I will work in you
and accomplish that which is pleasing in My sight as you
rely and depend upon My Son, Jesus. For it is not in your
own strength that you are changed, but as you depend
upon Me, I will work within you. I will create inside of you
the power and desire both to choose and to do what
pleases Me.

I will sanctify you and change you into everything I have called you to be. You can trust Me completely! I have called you to fulfill a special purpose. Rest assured that I will also bring it to pass. Yes, I will complete the work that I have begun in you!

Scripture Reading:

Romans 5:17	Hebrews 13:20-21
Philippians 2:13	1 Thessalonians 5:23-24

❧

Prayer:

Heavenly Father, I ask for Your grace to become effective in my life. I know I can't be all You want me to be in my own strength. I ask You to change me into Your image. Create in me the desire and ability to choose and to do what pleases You. You have called me to be like Jesus, and I know that as I trust You, You will accomplish this in my life. I want my life to be pleasing to You. Thank You, Lord, for Your grace. In Jesus' name,   *Amen.*

God Alone Can Satisfy

❧

He also has planted eternity in men's hearts and minds [a divinely implanted sense of a purpose working through the ages which nothing under the sun but God alone can satisfy].
Ecclesiastes 3:11 AMP

I have planted eternity in your mind and heart. This is a divinely implanted sense of purpose working through the ages, which nothing under the sun can satisfy except Me. Absolutely nothing can fill the void in your heart but Me alone.

You can search for happiness and satisfaction in relationships, in material things, in your job, in high positions, but you will never find it apart from Me.

My beloved, keep yourself from idols—from anything and everything that would occupy the place in your heart due Me, from any sort of substitute for Me that would take first place in your life.

I long to fill you with happiness and fulfillment. I long to fill your life with joy and peace, but I'm waiting for you to come to Me. I want to be your God, your Defender, your Refuge, your Guide, your Friend, your Everything.

Seek after Me alone, My child, and you will be completely satisfied. I will satisfy your every need and desire and fill your life with My blessings. I only want first place in your life.

Scripture Reading:

Ecclesiastes 3:11	1 John 5:21
Isaiah 30:18	Matthew 5:6
Psalm 37:4	

Prayer:

Heavenly Father, forgive me for looking to others to fulfill my needs. Forgive me for giving other things first place in my life. Forgive me for not completely trusting You. I run to You now, trusting You with every situation in my life. You are my Refuge, my Defender, my Guide, my Everything. I know that nothing this world offers can bring me the happiness and satisfaction that comes from an intimate relationship with You. I love you, Lord; You are my faithful Friend. In Jesus' name,   *Amen.*

God's Blessing

nd Promises

A Cornucopia of Blessings

*A faithful man shall
abound with blessings.*
Proverbs 28:20 KJV

*M*y child, do you know how much I long to fill
your life with My blessings? If you'll only seek
Me for help, I will strengthen and empower you to walk in
obedience to My Word. Then My blessings will overflow
into every area of your life.

Your children will be healthy and happy, and the food
you eat will bring nourishment to your body. You'll be
blessed wherever you go.

No obstacle will be too great because I will help you
overcome when others come against you.

I will command My blessings upon your storehouse,
and everything you do will succeed. I will give you
abundant prosperity, blessing all the work of your hands,
so you will be the lender, not the borrower. I'll promote you
to the top, and you'll be a great success! In fact, everyone
will see how I have blessed you, and you will speak to
them about My faithfulness.

This is My wonderful plan for you, so choose to obey My Word—but do not rely upon your own strength. Instead, trust Me to do the work in you, and I will give you the desire and power to walk in obedience to My Word. Then I will pour these blessings into your life. You will be a living testimony that I'm a God who gives good gifts to His children and rewards those who trust in Him.

Scripture Reading:

Isaiah 30:18   *Philippians 2:12-13*
Deuteronomy 28:1-13   *Psalm 92:15*

❧

Prayer:

Heavenly Father, I ask You to help me obey Your Word, for in it You have promised to fill my life with Your blessings. I want to be a doer of Your Word and not a hearer only. I ask You to effect Your work in me. Grant me the desire and ability to do what pleases You, for I know it is only by Your grace that I can walk in obedience to Your Word. I want to be a living testimony of Your goodness. In Jesus' name,   *Amen.*

Remember All His Benefits

Praise the LORD, O my soul,
and forget not all his benefits.
Psalm 103:2

Live a life of praise and thanksgiving, remembering all the benefits of being My child.

Not only do I forgive all your sins, but I heal your diseases as well. Whenever you are discouraged, know that I will strengthen you. I redeemed your life from the pit and destruction, crowning you with loving-kindness and tender mercies.

I satisfy your mouth with good things, so your youth is renewed, just as the eagle's. When you are oppressed, My righteousness and justice will vindicate you and put you back on your feet. I'm compassionate, gracious, and abounding in love toward you.

I'm a God of mercy and grace. I won't accuse you or be angry with you, for I don't treat you as your sins deserve. The truth is, My love for you is as high as the heavens are above the earth. And as far as the east is from the west, that's how far I have removed your sins from you.

I promise to bring salvation to your children and grandchildren because you put your complete trust in Me. So rejoice in My promises, as one who finds a great treasure. Then you will live and abide in My presence, and your joy will overflow.

Scripture Reading:

Psalm 103:1-22   Psalm 119:162

Psalm 16:11

❧

Prayer:

Heavenly Father, I praise and worship You with all my soul. I will keep my mind on You and remember the benefits of being Your child. You forgive all my sins and heal all my diseases. You redeem my life and crown me with Your love and mercy. You nourish me with good things, so my youth is renewed as the eagle's. You promised to bring salvation to my children, which is one of my greatest desires. You are so worthy of my praise. I love You, Lord, because I realize how very much You love me. I will rest secure in Your unfailing love. In Jesus' name,   *Amen.*

Jehovah Jireh—the Lord Who Provides

And my God will meet all your needs according to his glorious riches in Christ Jesus.
Philippians 4:19

J am your Heavenly Father, who delights in providing for you. Don't be anxious about having enough money to pay your bills. If you simply trust Me, I will take complete care of you. Besides, what good will worry bring? Does it benefit you to be concerned about your home, clothes, food, or finances?

Watch the birds of the air—they never lack because I make sure they are well provided for. If this is how I take care of even the tiniest bird, how much more will I provide for you? You are so much more valuable to Me. Yet aren't the animals and plants in this world well cared for? My child, never doubt a moment that I will provide much more for you.

So don't worry about material things, for the world spends so much time and energy seeking them, and I am well aware of what you need. Instead, seek first to promote My kingdom. Seek first My righteousness. This means to conform your life to My will in your thoughts, words, and actions. Then I will bless your life with all these other things. Yes, I will make sure that your every need is abundantly supplied.

Scripture Reading:

Psalm 35:27   Matthew 6:25-33

Romans 14:17   2 Timothy 2:22

Prayer:

Lord, forgive me for worrying about my finances; instead, help me remember that You are my Provider. I know that if You care for the tiniest bird, You will also provide for me. I will seek first Your kingdom and Your righteousness by trusting You to conform me to Jesus' image by the power of Your Spirit. As I seek to become more like Him in my thoughts, words, and actions, I know You will bless my life in all areas. I will trust You to abundantly supply my needs, just as You promised. In Jesus' name I pray,

Amen.

You Are Special to God

❧

*I am the Lord your God. . . . I have
put my words in your mouth and hidden
you safe within my hand. . . . I am the
one who says . . . "You are mine."*
Isaiah 51:15-16 TLB

*A*re you aware of just how much you mean to
Me? Not only did the angels in heaven rejoice
the day you became My child, but My heart, too, was filled
with delight. From that day on, as any father who's proud
of his child, I've kept your picture with Me, imprinted on
the very palms of My hands.

Take a look at all the incredible things I have created:
the sun, moon, and stars, for instance. And yet you are so
much more important to Me that they pale in comparison
to you. You are so dear to My heart that My thoughts
concerning you are too numerous to count.

There may be times in your life when others let you
down and forget about you. But know this: I will never
forget you because you belong to Me. You are mine forever;
I have hidden you within the safety of My hand, and I will
never let you out of My grasp. So never hesitate to call on

Me. I am your Heavenly Father, and I will always be
with you to help you whenever you need Me.

Scripture Reading:

Luke 15:7   Psalm 40:5

Psalm 46:1   Isaiah 49:15-16

~&

Prayer:

*Heavenly Father, how comforting it is to realize just how
special I am to You! My picture is engraved on the palms
of Your hands. I'm always on Your mind; You think about
me constantly. I now understand more than ever that You
will never fail me. Thank You, dear Lord, for always being
with me. I can trust You because I know that You will
never let me down. In Jesus' name,*   *Amen.*

Build Your House upon the Rock

❦

Through skillful and godly Wisdom is a house (a life, a home, a family) built, and by understanding it is established [on a sound and good foundation], And by knowledge shall its chambers [of every area] be filled with all precious and pleasant riches.
Proverbs 24:3-4 AMP

My Word is filled with My counsel and wisdom concerning every area of your life. As you follow My counsel, you'll be building your house upon a solid Rock. When the storms and trials of life come and the enemy tries to attack you, you'll stand strong on My Word and not be moved by any negative circumstance. You'll come through every trial victoriously.

However, if you choose to follow your own ways, you'll be building your house upon sinking sand. Then when the storms of life come against you or the enemy attacks you, your house will fall; My Word says that if you neglect My counsel, you'll bring destruction upon yourself.

My child, don't follow your own ways, but instead, seek My counsel and build your marriage, your family, and your life on the wisdom of My Word! It's a firm and sound foundation that will never fail you. As you follow My counsel, every area of your life will be filled with My blessings, and you will be completely satisfied.

Scripture Reading:

Matthew 7:24-27 Proverbs 13:13

❧

Prayer:

Heavenly Father, I want to build my life on the wisdom of Your Word. I know that following Your counsel will bring many blessings into my life. I will seek Your wisdom concerning my marriage, my children, my finances, my health, and my relationships; and I ask You to help me follow it. I'll build my house on the solid Rock. When trials come against me, I will look to You and Your Word for strength. Thank You for Your promise of victory. In Jesus' name, *Amen.*

Abundant Life

❧

*The thief cometh not, but for to steal,
and to kill, and to destroy: I am come
that they might have life, and that
they might have it more abundantly.*
John 10:10 KJV

You are My beloved child. My plan from the beginning has been to bless you, never to harm you. But you have an enemy—the devil—roams about like a roaring lion seeking someone to devour. He'd like nothing better than to deceive you into believing anything but the truth.

Don't believe the devil's lie that I would harm your life or that I am to blame for any negative circumstance he sends your way. When your faith is tempted and tried, don't accuse Me, for I do not create evil, nor do I tempt anyone. I am your Heavenly Father, and only that which is good and perfect comes from My hand.

I sent My Son, Jesus, that you might trust in Him and have an abundant life. He didn't come to condemn you, but to deliver and set you free.

It's My desire that you would enjoy life to the fullest. So in the midst of trials, resist the devil and his deceptions by trusting in My promises. Then you'll experience a life that is exceedingly, abundantly above all that you could ever hope or dream.

Scripture Reading:

Jeremiah 29:11   1 Peter 5:8-10

James 1:12-17   John 3:17

Ephesians 3:20

❧

Prayer:

Heavenly Father, thank You for sending Your Son, Jesus, that I might put my trust in Him and have an abundant life—one that exceeds my highest hopes and dreams. I know Your plan is to bless me—not to harm me. I know that when I experience trials, they don't come from You. But victory, deliverance, and salvation are Your good and perfect gifts. I know the devil wants to destroy me by convincing me of his lies. I will resist him by choosing instead to trust You to bring Your promises to pass in my life. Thank You, Lord, for Your many blessings. In Jesus' name,   *Amen.*

Persevering Prayer

*[Jesus] told them a parable to
the effect that they ought always
to pray and not to turn coward
(faint, lose heart, and give up).*
Luke 18:1 AMP

*D*on't become discouraged or give up in regard
to your prayers. Know that when you pray and
put your trust in Me, My power is at work bringing to
pass your heart's desire. Don't give up before you see
the answer.

Draw your strength from Me. Don't become worried or
anxious; because I am your Heavenly Father, and I will not
fail you nor forsake you.

There will be times when your faith will be tested,
and the situation that you've prayed about may seem to
worsen before it improves. But don't throw away your
steadfast confidence in Me, for your confident trust in Me
will be rewarded.

No matter how impossible the situation may seem,
don't become discouraged or quit trusting Me. Don't waver
or question My promise to you.

Instead, begin to praise and thank Me for what I have promised you in My Word. Then surely you will be strengthened and empowered by faith, knowing that what I have promised, I will perform.

Scripture Reading:

Hebrews 6:12-15	James 5:16
Deuteronomy 31:6	James 1:3-4
Hebrews 10:35	Romans 4:18-21

❧

Prayer:

Heavenly Father, I ask You for the strength to persevere when circumstances I've been praying about don't seem to be changing. I realize that I receive Your promises through trusting You and waiting patiently. So no matter how the situation may appear, I choose to continue to pray and trust You to bring to pass the desire of my heart. I won't waver or question Your promise. Instead, I will praise and thank You for the wonderful promises You have given to me. I put my confidence in You, Lord, because I know that You won't fail me. You are faithful to all Your promises. In Jesus' name,   *Amen.*

Your Heart's Desire

*Delight thyself also in the LORD;
and he shall give thee the desires of
thine heart. Commit thy way unto
the LORD; trust also in him;
and he shall bring it to pass.*
Psalm 37:4-5 KJV

I know everything about you and every desire of your heart—what you want for your children, your spouse, your marriage, and for yourself personally. Don't you realize that those desires are My will and plan for your life? If you'll only trust Me with all your heart, I will bring every one of them to pass.

Delight yourself in Me; find joy in your relationship with Me. Commit your every care into My hands; trust Me completely, and I will bring to pass every desire of your heart.

As you trust in My unfailing love, My power will be at work in your life. You will stand in awe as you watch Me perform things in your life far beyond what you could ever hope for or even imagine. You are My child, and it gives Me great pleasure to give you the desires of your heart.

Scripture Reading:

Psalm 139:1-2

Psalm 145:19

Ephesians 1:19

Ephesians 3:20

Deuteronomy 30:9

❧

Prayer:

Heavenly Father, I rejoice in Your promise to bring to pass every desire of my heart. Sometimes this seems impossible to me, but I know that nothing is impossible with You—all things are possible if I only believe. I understand what it is like for me to want to give my children the desires of their hearts; how much more do You want to do the same for me! Your love for me is so wonderful! I'm trusting You, Lord, to move powerfully on my behalf and to far exceed my highest prayers, desires, thoughts, hopes, and dreams in every area of my life. In Jesus' name, Amen.

Answered Prayer

❧

In solemn truth I tell you . . .
I am going to be with the Father.
You can ask him for anything, using
my name, and I will do it, for this
will bring praise to the Father
because of what I, the Son, will
do for you. Yes, ask anything,
using my name, and I will do it!
John 14:12-14 TLB

I'm your Heavenly Father, and I always speak the truth. I promise that if you ask Me for anything, using the name of Jesus, it will be done for you. You can be confident that if your request is in agreement with My will and plan, I will bring it to pass.

If you trust in Me, and My Word continues to live in your heart, you can ask whatever you will, and it shall be done for you.

Therefore, I tell you whatever your heart's desire, pray and ask Me to bring it to pass in your life. Then believe that you have received it.

I am able to do far beyond that which you could ever think to ask, far above your highest prayer. All things are possible if you will only believe.

Remember, you are My beloved child, and it gives Me great joy and delight to answer your prayers.

Scripture Reading:

1 John 5:14, 15	*John 15:7*
Mark 11:24	*Ephesians 3:20*
Mark 9:23	*Proverbs 15:8*

❧

Prayer:

Heavenly Father, thank You for Your promise to answer my prayers. I will put Your Word in my heart and pray it over my marriage, my children, myself, and others; for when I pray Your Word, I'm praying Your perfect will and plan for us. Because of Your promise, I am totally confident that You will watch over Your Word and perform it in our lives. In Jesus' name,   *Amen.*

The Prayer of Faith

*Now faith is the assurance of
things hoped for, the conviction
of things not seen.*
Hebrews 11:1 RSV

*W*hatever you ask for in prayer, having faith and truly believing, you will receive. When you pray and ask Me to do something for you, trust Me completely to bring it to pass. Don't doubt My promise to you. If you waver and doubt, you'll be like a wave of the sea, blown and tossed by the wind, and your prayers will be ineffective.

So ask in faith, and be confident of what you hope for; be convinced that it will take place, no matter how impossible this may seem. Remember that with Me nothing is ever impossible; all things are possible if you'll only trust and believe.

Don't you realize how much I love you? If you as an earthly parent want to give good gifts to your children, how much more do I as your Heavenly Father want to do good things for you? What is it that you desire of Me? Ask in faith, fully trusting Me to act on your behalf, and you will receive. Then your heart will overflow with joy.

Scripture Reading:

Matthew 21:21	James 1:5-7
Luke 1:37	Mark 9:23
Matthew 7:11	Matthew 20:32
John 16:24	

❧

Prayer:

Heavenly Father, forgive me for doubting You and Your faithfulness. I don't want to be like a wave of the sea, tossed to and fro with every negative circumstance that comes my way. I want to put my complete confidence in You. Help me trust You more. I'm trusting You, Lord, to do a work in me and bring to pass the answers to my prayers. I know that You are faithful to all Your promises. In Jesus' name,   *Amen.*

An Everlasting Covenant

*Is not my house right with God?
Has he not made with me an
everlasting covenant, arranged
and secured in every part? Will he
not bring to fruition my salvation
and grant me my every desire?*
2 Samuel 23:5

You are My beloved child, and I have made an everlasting covenant with you. My agreement with you is eternal and secure, sealed with the blood of Jesus. I will bring My salvation to fruition in your life and grant your every desire.

In the days of Noah, I swore that the waters would never again cover the earth. Now I have sworn not to rebuke you in My anger again. Though the mountains be shaken and the hills removed, My unfailing love for you will stand firm, and My covenant of peace will remain; because I have compassion on you.

I am your God of peace. Through the blood that sealed My everlasting covenant, I will strengthen you and equip you to carry out My will for your life. I will work in you to accomplish that which is pleasing in My sight. My only requirement of you is to daily trust and rely upon My Son, Jesus.

Scripture Reading:

Ezekiel 37:26	Genesis 12:2
2 Samuel 23:5	Hebrews 9:20
Isaiah 54:9-10	Hebrews 13:20-21
John 6:28-29	

❧

Prayer:

Heavenly Father, I completely trust You because of the covenant You have made with me. You have promised to bless my life through Your Son, Jesus. Your love is unfailing. Your promises are sure. I rejoice in Your salvation and promise to fulfill the desires of my heart. Your thoughts toward me are only loving and good. Thank You for Your promise to strengthen and equip me to carry out Your wonderful plan for my life. All You require is that I rely on Jesus in every moment of my life. As I do so, I know You will work in me and accomplish that which is pleasing in Your sight. In Jesus' name, Amen.

The Goodness of God

*May your priests, O LORD God,
be clothed with salvation, may your
saints rejoice in your goodness.*
2 Chronicles 6:41

*P*raise My name, My beloved; praise Me, for I am
good. Sing praises to My name. I have clothed
you with salvation, so rejoice in My goodness.

Oh, how great is My goodness toward you because you
love and obey Me! Everyone will watch as I pour out My
blessings on your life because you trust and reverence Me.

Celebrate My abundant goodness and joyfully sing of
My faithfulness, for I am righteous in all My ways and
gracious and merciful in all My works. I am near when you
call upon Me with sincerity and truth. I will hear your cry
and come to help you. I will also fulfill every desire of your
heart because you put your trust in Me. I will open up My
hand and provide for your every need; every good and
perfect gift comes from Me.

You can be completely confident, My beloved, that you
will see My goodness in the land of the living, for surely

My goodness and mercy will follow you all the days of your life.

Scripture Reading:

Psalm 135:3	2 Chronicles 6:41
Psalm 31:19	Psalm 145:7, 16-19
James 1:17	Psalm 27:13
Psalm 23:6	

❧

Prayer:

Heavenly Father, You have clothed me with salvation; therefore, I will rejoice in Your goodness. I will celebrate Your abundant goodness and joyfully sing of Your faithfulness. What would become of me if I did not believe that I would see Your goodness in my life? You hear me when I cry and come to my rescue. You open Your hand and provide for my every need. Your blessings abound toward me, and Your love is unfailing. Surely Your goodness and mercy will follow me all of my days. In Jesus' name, *Amen.*

Seek after God

He is the rewarder of those who
earnestly and diligently seek Him.
Hebrews 11:6 AMP

*G*et to know Me, My child; worship and serve Me
with a clean heart and a willing mind; because I
see your heart, and I know your every thought. If you seek
after Me, you will find Me.

I look down from heaven on humanity to see if there
are any who understand, any who seek Me. My eyes run to
and fro throughout the whole earth, desiring to show
myself strong in the lives of those whose hearts trust Me.

So seek after Me as though you were searching for
silver, and search for My wisdom as though you were
looking for a hidden treasure; then you will understand
what it means to truly reverence Me, and you will know
Me more intimately.

When you diligently seek Me, I will answer you; I will
deliver you from all your fears. When you look to Me, you
will be radiant; your face will never be covered with shame.

Search for My instruction and reverently fear Me. As long as you seek Me with all your heart, I will cause you to prosper; I will reward you when you earnestly and diligently pursue Me.

Scripture Reading:

2 Chronicles 28:9   Psalm 53:2

2 Chronicles 16:9   Proverbs 2:4-5

Psalm 34:4-15   2 Chronicles 26:5

Hebrews 11:6

❧

Prayer:

Heavenly Father, I will seek after You by studying Your Word and searching for Your wisdom as though I am searching for a hidden treasure. I want to understand what it means to truly reverence You. I want to know You more fully. There is great reward in pursuing You. For when I look to You and trust You with all of my heart, You will cause me to prosper in every area of my life; that is Your plan for me. I love You, Lord; help me to be more like You. In Jesus' name,   *Amen.*

A Thankful Heart

Be joyful always; pray continually; give
thanks in all circumstances, for this
is God's will for you in Christ Jesus.
1 Thessalonians 5:16-18

*E*nter My gates with thanksgiving and My courts
with praise; give thanks to Me and praise My
name, and I will fill you with joy in My presence.

Through My Son, Jesus, constantly offer up to Me a
sacrifice of praise, which is the fruit of your lips thankfully
acknowledging, confessing, and glorifying My name; with
such sacrifices I am well pleased.

When you live a life of praise and thanksgiving, you
glorify Me, and you prepare the way for Me to show you
My salvation in every situation.

So rejoice in Me and pray continually, giving thanks to
My name, for this is My will for you in Christ Jesus. Then I
will show myself strong in your life because your heart is
perfect toward Me. All who see you prospering in life will
recognize and acknowledge that you are My child whom I
have richly blessed.

P. S. GOD LOVES YOU!

Scripture Reading:

Psalm 100:4-5   Psalm 16:11

Hebrews 13:15-16   Psalm 50:23

1 Thessalonians 5:16-18   Ephesians 5:19-20

2 Chronicles 16:9   Isaiah 61:9

❧

Prayer:

Heavenly Father, I praise and thank You for all the wonderful promises You have given me. I rejoice in Your promises, as one who finds great treasure. I thank You so much for sending Jesus to die for me so that I might have a wonderful, abundantly blessed life. You are so loving and good. You have promised to bless my life in every way. This reveals to me just how much You love me. I love You, Lord, because You first loved me. I know that when I have a thankful heart, it prepares the way for You to shower me with Your blessings and show me Your salvation. In Jesus' name,   *Amen.*

The Love of Christ

*As the Father has loved me, so have
I loved you. Now remain in My love.*
John 15:9

Y ou are precious to Me because I love you. I have
chosen you for myself, and you are My
treasured possession.

I am always near you. When I look at you, I rejoice
with singing, for My heart delights in you. As a bridegroom
rejoices over his bride, so I rejoice over you.

How beautiful you are, My beloved! Oh, how beautiful!
There is no flaw in you. You have stolen My heart, My
bride; you have stolen My heart with one glance of your
eyes. I have taken you to the banqueting hall, and My
banner over you is love. I gather you in My arms and carry
you close to My heart. My left arm is under your head, and
My right arm embraces you. You are Mine, and I am yours.
So rest secure in Me, My beloved, for I surround you with
My loving care. You are the one I love; come rest between
My shoulders.

As the Father has loved Me, so have I loved you. Now remain in My love. You can be confident, My beloved; there is absolutely nothing that could ever keep Me from loving you, for you are the apple of My eye.

Scripture Reading:

Isaiah 43:4	Psalm 135:4
Zephaniah 3:17	Isaiah 62:5
Song of Songs 4:1,7,9	Song of Songs 2: 6,16
Isaiah 40:11	John 15:9
Deuteronomy 33:12	Psalm 17:8
Romans 8:39	

Prayer:

Lord Jesus, I love You with all my heart, for You have proven Your love for me. You gather me in Your arms and carry me close to Your heart. I will rest secure in You, for You surround me with Your loving care. I am confident that nothing will ever separate me from Your great love. In Jesus' name,   Amen.

Waiting on God

*The Lord is wonderfully good
to those who wait for him, to
those who seek for him. It is both good
to hope and wait quietly for the
salvation of the Lord.*
Lamentations 3:25-26 TLB

I am wonderfully good to those who wait for Me, to those who seek after Me. It is good to wait patiently for My salvation. My eyes are upon you as you trust in Me, as you wait for Me and hope in My unfailing love.

My ears pay attention to your prayers. When you lay your requests before Me, wait in expectation. For if I did not spare My own Son, but gave Him up for you, will I not also freely and graciously give you all things? No good thing will I withhold from you when your walk before Me is blameless.

I long to be gracious to you; I rise up to show you compassion. I am a God of justice, and I will surely bless you when you confidently wait for Me.

So, be still before Me and wait patiently for Me to act. You will never be disappointed when you put your trust in Me. Wait for Me, My child, and put your hope in My Word.

Trust in My unfailing love, and surely your heart will rejoice in My salvation.

Scripture Reading:

Lamentations 3:25-26	Psalm 33:18
1 Peter 3:12	Psalm 5:3
Romans 8:32	Psalm 84:11
Isaiah 30:18	Psalm 37:7
Isaiah 49:23	Psalm 130:5-8
Psalm 13:5	

❧

Prayer:

Heavenly Father, I will wait patiently for Your salvation. I put my hope in Your unfailing love. When I lay my requests before You, I will wait in expectation, for You long to be gracious to me and answer my every prayer. I put my hope in Your Word, fully trusting You to fulfill Your promise in my life. I will wait patiently for You to act. I know that You will never disappoint me when I put my trust in You. In Jesus' name,   *Amen.*

Delight in God's Word

～

But his delight is in the law of the
LORD, and on his law he meditates day
and night. He is like a tree planted
by streams of water, which yields its
fruit in season and whose leaf does
not wither. Whatever he does prospers.
Psalm 1:2-3

I will bless your life in every way when you delight
in My Word, meditating upon it day and night.
You will be like a tree planted by streams of living water.
Love, joy, peace, patience, kindness, goodness, humility,
faithfulness, and self-control will be the fruit of your life;
and everything you do will prosper and come to maturity.

So rejoice in following My ways, as you would rejoice
in great riches. Meditate on My commands, and have deep
reverence toward Me. Delight in My laws, and do not
neglect My Word.

My laws are perfect; they will restore and refresh your
soul. My counsel is trustworthy; it will make you wise. My
promises are true; they will bring joy to your heart. My
commands are pure; they will bring light to your eyes.

Through them you are warned, but in keeping them there is great reward.

If you'll obey My word and reverently worship Me, you'll spend your days in prosperity, and your years will be filled with pleasantness and joy.

Scripture Reading:

Psalm 1:2-3   Psalm 119:14-16

Psalm 19:7-11   Job 36:11

❧

Prayer:

Heavenly Father, I will delight myself in Your Word by meditating and thinking upon it day and night. I rejoice in following Your ways, as one rejoices in great riches. Your ways are perfect, and Your promises are sure. There is great reward in obeying You. I ask You to give me the grace to follow Your ways. I love You, Lord, and I will follow You all the days of my life. In Jesus' name,

Amen.

God Will Guide You

❧

I will instruct you (says the Lord)
and guide you along the best pathway
for your life; I will advise you
and watch your progress.
Psalm 32:8 TLB

I will guide you along the best pathway for your
life. I will counsel you and watch over your every
step. I am the Lord your God, who teaches you what is
best for you and who directs you in the way you should go.

I will guide you in the way of wisdom and lead you
down the right path. When you walk, your steps will not be
hampered; when you run, you will not fall.

I am your Rock and your Fortress. For the sake of My
name, I will lead and guide you.

I will lead you by the way you have not known; along
unfamiliar paths I will guide you; I will turn the darkness
into light before you and make the rough places smooth.
These are the things I'm determined to do for you. I will
never fail you.

I walk before you and call your name. I lead you, and
you follow Me because you know My voice; the voice of a
stranger you will not follow.

I am your God forever and ever! I will be your Guide even to the end.

Scripture Reading:

Psalm 32:8	Isaiah 48:17
Proverbs 4:11-12	Psalm 31:3
Isaiah 42:16	John 10:3-5
Psalm 48:14	

❧

Prayer:

Heavenly Father, I ask You to guide me toward the best pathway for my life. I want to follow Your perfect plan for me. When I am confused about decisions that need to be made, I will look to You for guidance. I ask You to direct my heart in the right direction and keep me on the straight and narrow path. Thank You for Your promises. Because of them, I can be confident that You will never fail to help me make the right choices. In fact, You will lead me toward Your will in every situation. In Jesus' name, *Amen.*

A New and Better Covenant

⁓

Jesus has become the
guarantee of a better covenant.
Hebrews 7:22

*J*esus is your guarantee of a better covenant. This covenant is superior to the old one because it is founded upon better promises.

This is the covenant I have made with you through My Son, Jesus: I am your God, and you are My child. I have forgiven all your sins, and I have completely forgotten them. I have given you a new heart and put a new spirit in you; I have removed from you your heart of stone and given you a heart of love. I have put My Spirit in you to cause you to follow My Word and to create in you the desire and power to obey it. This is for your own good and for the good of your children after you.

I have made an everlasting covenant with you: I will never be angry with you or rebuke you again. I will never stop doing good to you. I will inspire you to fear Me, so you will follow Me and won't ever turn away. I will rejoice with all of My heart in doing good for you, and I will give you all the blessings I have promised. All that I require of you is this: you must daily trust and rely upon Jesus and the promises I have given you through Him.

Scripture Reading:

Hebrews 7:22
Ezekiel 36:26-27
Isaiah 54:9-10
John 6:28-29

Hebrews 8:6,10,12
Philippians 2:13
Jeremiah 32:38-42

Prayer:

Heavenly Father, I rejoice in the covenant You have made with me through Your Son, Jesus. I realize that all I must do to partake of Your covenant promises is daily trust and rely upon Jesus. As I do so, You will give me the power and ability to obey Your Word, and You will bless me with all that You have promised. I choose to believe the promises that You have given me through Jesus. It is wonderful to know that You rejoice in blessing me. It delights Your heart to fulfill Your promises in my life. You have proven Your great love for me by sending Jesus so that I might partake of Your wonderful blessings. I can trust You, Lord, because You only want the very best for my life, and You are faithful to Your covenant promises. In Jesus' name,   Amen.

Redeemed through Christ

❧

Christ redeemed us from the curse of the law by becoming a curse for us. . . . He redeemed us in order that the blessing given to Abraham might come to the Gentiles through Christ Jesus, so that by faith we might receive the promise of the Spirit.
Galatians 3:13-14

*T*he spirit of life in Christ Jesus has freed you from sin and its consequences. In trusting Jesus you have redemption through His blood. Your sins are forgiven, and My grace is poured out upon you.

Jesus has freed you from the curses of the law, including a bad marriage, rebellious children, financial lack, sickness, depression, a worried and anxious heart, failure, and defeat. He has paid the price with His own blood to deliver you from these curses when you put your complete trust in Him.

As you trust your Redeemer with all your heart, the blessings I promised to Abraham will come to you. These blessings include the Spirit of grace, salvation of your family, a happy marriage, blessed children, financial abundance, healing and health, answered prayer, joy, peace, love, success, protection, and victory. No matter the number, My promises are "Yes!" and "Amen!" in your life when you put your trust in Jesus.

Lift your voice to Me in praise for your redemption and humbly receive all I have provided for you through the blood of Jesus. When you do this, My promised blessings will flood your life.

Scripture Reading:

Romans 8:2	*Ephesians 1:7-8*
Galatians 3:13-14	*Deuteronomy 28:14-68*
1 Corinthians 1:20	*Psalm 50:23*

Prayer:

Lord Jesus, You are my Redeemer, Deliverer, Savior, and Lord. I trust You completely. I praise You and thank You for redeeming me from sin and all its consequences. You have purchased my freedom from the curses of the law so that the promises given to Abraham might come into my life. I have done nothing to deserve Your overwhelming goodness and amazing grace. I humbly receive all You have provided for me. Your faithfulness is wonderful, and I will praise You all the days of my life. In Jesus' name,

Amen.

Saved by Grace

For it is by grace you have been saved, through faith—and this not from yourselves, it is the gift of God.
Ephesians 2:8

*M*y beloved child, in order to satisfy the great and wonderful and intense love that I have for you, I saved you by My grace. I delivered you from My judgement and made you an heir to all My promises through your simple trust in Christ. I did this to clearly demonstrate the immeasurable riches of My free grace and goodness of heart toward you.

I saved you and called you to live a holy life—not because of any good works you have done, but because of My purpose and grace.

You will never be declared righteous in My sight by trying to be good enough. I made you righteous—perfect and without fault—when you put your trust in Jesus.

You can never be worthy of My blessings by depending on your good works, but only through trusting in Christ. This life you live on the earth, you live by daily trusting in My Son, Jesus, who loved you and gave Himself up for you.

So don't set aside My grace by trying to be good enough to please Me, for if righteousness could be gained through your good works, My Son, Jesus, died in vain.

Scripture Reading:

Ephesians 2:4-8   2 Timothy 1:9
Romans 3:20,22   Galatians 2:16, 20-21

❧

Prayer:

Heavenly Father, thank You for saving me by Your grace. You have delivered me from judgement and made me an heir of Your salvation. You did this, not because I was good enough, but because of Your wonderful grace. I now know what truly pleases You. It is not all of my good works, but my faith and trust in Jesus that make me righteous before You and an heir to all of Your promises. I can never be good enough in myself, but I praise You for making me righteous through my faith in Christ. I can live a holy life, not by trying, but by trusting in Jesus to do the work within me. Thank You, Father, for pouring Your grace upon my life. It truly is amazing! In Jesus' name,

Amen.

Jesus is Coming Soon

He who is the faithful witness to all these things says, "Yes, I am coming soon!" Amen! Come, Lord Jesus!
Revelation 22:20 NLT

*M*y Beloved, don't let your heart be troubled. Instead, trust in Me. In heaven, where My Father lives, there are many wonderful, beautiful homes, and the streets are paved with pure gold. I am preparing a place for you. When everything is ready, I will come retrieve you to be with Me forever.

I want to remind you that in the last days scoffers will arise. They will say, "Where is this coming He promised?" They will even laugh at you and make fun of those who believe I will come again. But remember this, My child— with Me a day is like a thousand years.

I'm not really slow in My promised return, even though it may seem that way. For I'm waiting because I want no one to perish; I want everyone to come to repentance.

I am telling you the truth. Those who are still alive when I return will not rise to meet Me ahead of those who are in the graves. For I will come down from heaven with a mighty shout, with the voice of the archangel, and with the trumpet-call of God, and those who have fallen asleep in death will rise first. Then those who are still alive on the earth will be caught up with them in the clouds to meet Me, and you will remain with Me forever. So be encouraged and know that I surely am coming for you very soon.

Scripture Reading:

John 14:1-3   Revelations 21:21

2 Peter 3:3-9   1 Thessalonians 4:15-18

Revelations 22:20

Prayer:

Lord Jesus, I am ready for Your return. I am watching and waiting because I know that Your promises are sure. I am encouraged to know that those I love who have gone on before me will be present with me at Your return, and we will live in heaven together forever. I rejoice in Your promise. In Jesus' name,   *Amen.*

God's Great and Precious Promises

⟿

Through these he has given us
his very great and precious promises,
so that through them you may
participate in the divine nature
and escape the corruption in the
world caused by evil desires.
2 Peter 1:4

*T*he devil's plan is to steal, kill, and destroy you, but I sent My Son, Jesus, so you might enjoy life to the fullest. His very purpose in coming was to provide an abundant life for you.

Through your knowledge of Jesus, I have given you everything you need to experience this abundant life. Through Him I have granted you My exceedingly great and precious promises, so that through them you might partake of My divine nature and escape the devil's plan for your life.

I have bound myself with an oath so that you can be very sure I will fulfill My promises in your life. I did this so that when you cling to the hope that I have offered you in My Word, you will be greatly encouraged because it is impossible for Me to lie.

No matter how many promises I have made, they all can be answered through trusting in Jesus.

As you trust Him with each day's problems, your life will glorify Me. You will become a living testimony proving that I am a good and loving God who is faithful to all My promises.

Scripture Reading:

John 10:10   2 Peter 1:3-4
Hebrews 6:17-18   2 Corinthians 1:20
Psalm 92:15

❧

Prayer:

Heavenly Father, thank You for sending Jesus so that I might have an abundant, blessed life. Because of Jesus, You have given me such wonderful promises. You have bound yourself with an oath assuring that You will fulfill them in my life. When I cling to the hope You have offered me in Your Word, I am greatly encouraged because I know You cannot lie. Your answer is always "Yes" when I put my trust in Jesus. Therefore, I confidently respond to Your promises by saying, "Amen, so be it in my life!" I want my life to glorify You and be a living testimony of proof that You are faithful to all Your promises. I am trusting You, Lord, to bring to pass what You have promised me. In Jesus' name,   *Amen.*

Supernatural Favor

For whoever finds me [Wisdom]
finds life and draws forth and
obtains favor from the Lord.
Proverbs 8:35 AMP

*D*on't let mercy, kindness, and truth leave you, but write them on the tablet of your heart. Then My favor will surround you, and you will be favored by others.

Commit every one of your cares and concerns into My hands and trust Me completely. Then I will make your uprightness go forth as the light and your righteousness shine as the noonday sun.

I will open doors of opportunity for you and cause you to find favor and kindness with those in high positions.

So put your trust in Me. Sing and shout for joy because I have made a covering over you and defend you. Be in high spirits and rejoice, for I will surely bless you and surround you with My favor as a shield.

I will command My blessings upon you and upon all the work of your hands. You will be blessed everywhere you go.

Others will see My favor upon you, and they will acknowledge that you are My child whom I have richly blessed.

Scripture Reading:

Proverbs 3:3-4	Psalm 34:5-6
Revelations 3:8	Daniel 1:9
Acts 7:9-10	Psalm 5:11-12
Deuteronomy 28:6,8	Isaiah 61:9
Proverbs 5:11-12	

❧

Prayer:

Heavenly Father, I won't let mercy, kindness, and truth depart from me. I will write them on the tablet of my heart. I give You my cares and concerns, and I trust that You will shine Your favor upon me. I rejoice in Your promise, for surely You will bless my life and surround me with the shield of Your favor. I truly want to praise and thank You for opening doors of opportunity and giving me favor with those in high positions. Your promises are too wonderful for me. Lord, I rest secure in Your faithfulness. In Jesus' name,   *Amen.*

God Longs to Bless You

*Yet the LORD longs to be gracious to
you; he rises to show you compassion.
For the LORD is a God of justice.
Blessed are all who wait for him!*
Isaiah 30:18

My child, when you go through hard times, know that I am with you. I will never give up on you. You may wonder where I am, but I have promised I will never leave you nor forsake you. I am right here waiting for you to turn your heart completely toward Me.

If you will only look to Me and rest in Me, I will bring victory into your life. If you will simply trust Me, you will be filled with My strength.

I long to be gracious toward you. I lift myself up that I may have mercy on you and show you My loving-kindness. I'm a God of justice, and I bless those who put their trust in Me.

I require your trust and your confidence—that's all I ask of you; I'm a jealous God, and I want all of your heart, not just part. I want your undivided attention and your unbroken companionship. I want you to put your hope in

Me alone: When you choose to do this, you will see My power at work in your life, and you will shine with My glory and walk in complete victory.

Scripture Reading:

Isaiah 43:1-3   Isaiah 30:15,18

Ephesians 1:19

❧

Prayer:

Heavenly Father, forgive me for not putting my complete trust in You. I realize I have put my hope in things other than You and this has brought much heartache and discouragement into my life. I choose today to put my hope and confidence in You alone and the promises of Your Word. I know that You long to bless my life. Your only requirement of me is that I give You my complete trust by keeping my mind on You. I look to You, Heavenly Father, and I trust You to bring Your wonderful plan and purpose to pass in my life. In Jesus' name,   *Amen.*

Heaven is Your Home

In my Father's house are many mansions: if it were not so, I would have told you. I go to prepare a place for you.
John 14:2 KJV

I love you, and I have prepared an eternal home for you that is beyond what you could ever dream or imagine. Never look at death as a loss, for it is a great gain because to be in heaven with Me is far better than to be on this earth.

In heaven there are no more tears; never again will you experience sorrow, mourning, grief, or pain. You will never again experience sickness or death. Instead you will have happiness, health, prosperity, peace, and love that lasts for an eternity.

The streets are paved with pure gold. The gates are made of pearls, and I have built the most beautiful mansions ever imaginable. In fact, I have built one just for you and those you love.

A river of life, sparkling like crystal, flows out from My throne, and beside it grow trees of life that produce the most delicious fruit you've ever tasted.

There is no night nor any need for a sun or moon because My radiant splendor and glory illuminate all of heaven—Jesus is the lamp. Yes, in heaven you and all of My children will reign as kings forever.

Scripture Reading:

John 14:2   Philippians 1:21,23
Revelations 21:4, 18-24   Revelations 22:1-5

❧

Prayer:

Heavenly Father, Your love for me is so great. You have prepared such a wonderful place for me and my family to spend eternity. I am so thankful that You sent Jesus to die for my sins so that I could spend eternity in heaven with You. I will love, worship, and praise You all the days of my life. The most wonderful promise You have given me is the promise of an eternal home in heaven. Thank You for reminding me just how wonderful it will be. I love You, Lord, because You first loved me. In Jesus' name,

Amen.

Seek God's Wisdom

*He is the rewarder of those who
earnestly and diligently seek Him [out].*
Hebrews 11:6 AMP

*M*y child, if you will listen to My Word, storing up My commandments as treasure; if you will be attentive to skillful and godly wisdom, applying all your powers to the quest for it; yes, if you cry out for insight and raise your voice for understanding, seeking wisdom like silver and searching for it like hidden treasure; then you will come to fear Me with worship and reverence, and you will begin to know Me.

For if you find wisdom and gain understanding, you will be blessed because the gaining of wisdom is better than silver, and its profit than fine gold. Skillful and godly wisdom is more precious than rubies, and nothing you desire can be compared to it.

Wisdom holds the length of days in its right hand, and in its left hand are riches and honor. The ways of wisdom are highways of pleasantness, and all its paths are peace.

Wisdom is a tree of life to those who gain understanding, and if you hold it fast, it will bring you happiness.

Scripture Reading:

Proverbs 2:1-5   Proverbs 3:13-18

❧

Prayer:

Heavenly Father, I will seek Your wisdom by studying and thinking upon Your Word. I ask for insight and understanding as I daily read my Bible. Impart to me Your wonderful wisdom, so that I might do what You have instructed and receive your wonderful blessings in my life. I want to do things Your way and not my own. Help me, Lord, to be obedient to Your Word. In Jesus' name,

Amen.

The Rewards of Following Wisdom

~&

*The fear of the Lord is pure, enduring
forever. The ordinances of the Lord are
sure and altogether righteous. By them
is your servant warned; in keeping
them there is great reward.*
Psalm 19:9,11

*M*y child, as you learn to reverently fear Me,
you will begin to know wisdom. Don't lose
sight of Godly wisdom and discretion. Hold tight to them,
for they fill you with life and bring you honor and respect.
They keep you safe on your way and keep your feet from
stumbling. You can lie down without fear and enjoy
pleasant dreams. You need not be afraid of disaster or the
destruction that comes upon the wicked, for you know that
My ways will protect you.

Listen to me and consent and submit to my sayings.
Keep Godly wisdom and discretion at the center of your
heart. They are life to those who find them, healing and
health to all their flesh.

If you value wisdom, hold it in esteem; embrace it, and it will bring you honor. It shall give to your head a wreath of gracefulness; a crown of beauty and glory will it deliver to you. Listen to what I say, My child, and the years of your life shall be many.

Scripture Reading:

Proverbs 3:21-23   Proverbs 4:8-10,20-22

Proverbs 9:10

Prayer:

Heavenly Father, the reward for following Your wisdom is a wonderful, blessed life. How I want to be blessed by You! Help me follow Your wisdom and correct me quickly when I fail. I love You, Lord, with all my heart, and I want my life to be pleasing to You. In Jesus' name,   Amen.

God is Your Defender

*But no weapon that is formed against
you shall prosper, and every tongue
that shall rise against you in judgment
you shall show to be in the wrong.
This [peace, righteousness, security,
triumph over opposition] is the
heritage of the servants of the Lord . . .
this is the righteousness or the
vindication which they obtain from Me
[this is that which I impart to them as
their justification], says the Lord.*
Isaiah 54:17 AMP

My child, you will have others come against you,
but remember My promise: No weapon formed
against you shall succeed, and every tongue that speaks
out against you in judgement you shall show to be in the
wrong. This triumph over opposition is your inheritance.
This is the vindication that you will receive from Me.

If I am on your side, who can succeed at coming against
you? I will defend, protect, and avenge you when you call out
to Me. I will not delay help on your behalf. I tell you the
truth; I will defend and protect and avenge you speedily.

I am your High Tower and Defense, your God in whom
you can take refuge.

P. S. GOD LOVES YOU!

Commit your cares into My hands and trust Me.
Depend on and be confident in Me, and I will make your
uprightness shine as the dawn and your righteousness
as the noonday sun; all who come against you will see
My glory shining brightly in your life.

Scripture Reading:

Isaiah 54:17	Romans 8:31
Luke 18:7-8	Psalm 94:22
Psalm 37:4-6	Isaiah 60:2

Prayer:

*Heavenly Father, I look to You as my Defender, my Rock,
and my Fortress in whom I confidently trust. Although
others may come against me, I know my vindication lies
in You. You will cause my uprightness to shine as the
dawn and my righteousness as the noonday sun. They will
see Your glory in my life. For if You are on my side, who
can be against me? I love You, Lord; thank You for Your
promise of victory. In Jesus' name,*   *Amen.*

God's Plan fo

Your Life

Financial Blessings

*Ye that fear the LORD, trust in the LORD:
he is their help and their shield. The
LORD hath been mindful of us: he will
bless us. . . . He will bless them that
fear the LORD, both small and great.
The LORD shall increase you more
and more, you and your children.*
Psalm 115:11-14 KJV

I am your Heavenly Father, and I'm always
thinking about you. I will bless your life when
you trust and reverence Me.

My beloved, as you live a life of worship and
thanksgiving toward Me, I will cause you to increase more
and more in every area of your life. You and your children
will partake in My abundant blessings.

Honor and worship Me by giving Me the first part of
all your income, and I will fill your storage places with
plenty. You will always have more than enough.

Put Me first in your finances; ask Me for wisdom, and
I will give you witty ideas that will bring financial blessings
into your life. Be a faithful and wise steward over the little
that you have, and I promise to make you a ruler over

much. You are My child, and it delights My heart greatly to increase you more and more.

Scripture Reading:

Psalm 50:14,23	*Proverbs 3:9-10*
James 1:5	*Proverbs 8:12*
Psalm 35:27	*Matthew 25:23*

❧

Prayer:

Heavenly Father, thank You for Your promise to increase me more and more in every area of my life. I know that this is Your plan for me. Help me trust You with my finances. I will worship and honor You by giving You the first part of my income. I rejoice in Your promise to fill my bank accounts with plenty and increase my income more and more. I ask You for wisdom, to give me clever ideas that will bring financial blessings into my life. Help me be a faithful and wise steward over what You have given me. I love You, Lord. You are so good to me. In Jesus' name,

Amen.

A Life of Giving

Give, and it shall be given unto you;
good measure, pressed down, and
shaken together, and running over,
shall men give into your bosom.
For with the same measure
that ye mete withal it shall
be measured to you again.
Luke 6:38 KJV

*M*y plan for your life is to bless you, so you can be a blessing to others.

When you give freely, you will gain even more, but if you withhold what you have, you will live in lack. Remember this: if you give little of your income to My work, then you'll receive little of My blessings. But if you'll give generously, so My blessings can come to others, I promise that My abundant blessings will overflow toward you as well.

Always give with a cheerful and willing heart. I take great pleasure in seeing you give joyfully. For when you give generously out of love, I will make all grace abound to you. You will not only have enough money to meet your own needs, but you'll also have plenty left over to continue giving to others.

Yes, because you fully trust Me, I will increase your finances, enabling you to give more into My kingdom. I promise to make you wealthy in every aspect of your life, so you can be generous to others in every area of their lives. Your life will glorify Me as those whom you have blessed thank Me for your generosity. They will indeed see My surpassing grace and loving-kindness in you.

Scripture Reading:

Genesis 12:2   Proverbs 11:24
2 Corinthians 9:6-15

❧

Prayer:

Heavenly Father, I ask You to grant me a pure heart that delights in being a blessing to others. I love You, Lord, and I want my actions to please You. Thank You for Your promise to bless me abundantly when I give with a joyful heart. Thank You for revealing Your plan for me to live in abundance, lacking nothing. I rejoice in Your promise to give all grace to me, so I can give generously to every good work. Thank You, Lord, for Your faithfulness. In Jesus' name, Amen.

God's Plan for You

"For I know the plans I have for you,"
declares the Lord, "plans to prosper
you and not to harm you, plans to
give you hope and a future."
Jeremiah 29:11

J have a wonderful plan for your life, a plan to
prosper you and in no way harm you, a plan to
give you hope for your future. I wish above all things that
you would prosper in every way and be in perfect health,
even as your soul prospers.

I didn't create you to be a failure. I created you to be a
success! Listen to My Word; follow My wisdom, and I'll
show you how to become a success in every area of your
life—in your family, in your profession, and even in your
finances. As your Heavenly Father, I love to bless you! I
promise that if you'll declare My Word to be true in your
life and think upon it day and night, and if you'll trust Me
to help you walk in My ways, you'll be like a tree firmly
planted by streams of living water, and you'll bear much
fruit. My blessings will overtake you, and you'll prosper
and be successful in everything you do.

Scripture Reading:

3 John 2   Deuteronomy 30:8-9

Joshua 1:8   Psalm 1:1-3

⌁

Prayer:

Heavenly Father, thank You for revealing Your wonderful plan for my life. I know that You don't want me to fail. Your desire is for me to prosper in every way. Therefore, I will declare Your Word to be true in my life and think upon it day and night. I ask You to help me follow Your counsel concerning my marriage, my parenting, my job, my health, my finances, and my relationships. Because of Your promises, I know that seeking You in these things will bring Your plan of prosperity into every area of my life. In Jesus' name,   Amen.

Divine Health

A *calm* and *undisturbed mind* and *heart*
are the life and *health of the body,*
but envy, jealousy, and *wrath are*
like rottenness of the bones.
Proverbs 14:30 AMP

*M*y child, guard your heart with all diligence, for
out of it flows the issues of life. Don't allow
anger, unforgiveness, resentment, jealousy, worry, or
offenses to remain in your heart, for they will bring
sickness to your body. But if you'll renew your mind in My
Word and be careful to follow My wisdom, you'll walk in
divine health.

Don't be wise in your own eyes, thinking that your
ways are better or easier than Mine. If you neglect My
counsel, you'll bring destruction on yourself, but if you'll
reverence Me and follow My ways, I will reward you. So
turn entirely away from evil and choose to trust and
reverence Me; this will bring health to your body and
nourishment to your bones.

If you've allowed any sin to enter your heart, confess
it to Me, and I will forgive you and cleanse you from all

unrighteousness. Then praise and worship Me, remembering that I am the Lord your God, who forgives all your sins and heals all your diseases.

Scripture Reading:

Proverbs 4:20-23   Proverbs 3:7-8

Proverbs 13:13   Psalm 103:2-3

1 John 1:9

❧

Prayer:

Heavenly Father, I will be diligent to guard my heart. I won't allow anything to enter in that is not pleasing to You. Please forgive me for the times I haven't guarded my heart. Help me to walk in Your ways and choose Your wisdom over my own. I know this will bring life and health to me because You have promised it in Your Word. Thank You, Lord, for forgiving all my sins and healing all my sicknesses. In Jesus' name,   *Amen.*

The Salvation
of Your Family

"*Believe in the Lord Jesus, and you will
be saved—you and your household.*
Acts 16:31

*D*on't worry about your family's salvation.
Instead, trust in Jesus and you—and your
family—will be saved.

Your loved ones who are not yet saved have been
blinded by the enemy from the truth of My Son, Jesus.

I urge you to make requests, prayers, and thanksgiving
for them. This pleases Me, for I want them to be saved and
know the truth.

Be assured that as you pray for your family, I will
deliver them from darkness and bring them into the
kingdom of My Son. Yes, I will deliver them through the
cleanness of your hands.

Never allow their attitudes or actions to cause you to
doubt that they'll be saved because My grace is sufficient
for them. When you pray and completely trust in Me, My
tremendous power will work in their lives. I will exert My
holy influence upon their minds, wills, and emotions and
turn their hearts toward Christ.

So enter into rest by simply praising and thanking Me for their deliverance. Surely you will see them come to Jesus.

Scripture Reading:

2 Corinthians 4:3-4	1 Timothy 2:1-4
Colossians 1:13	Job 22:30
James 5:16	John 6:44
2 Corinthians 1:12	Psalm 50:23

❧

Prayer:

Heavenly Father, I ask You to send laborers across the path of each unsaved member of my family. As they hear the Gospel of Jesus, open their eyes to the truth. I ask that You would draw them to You and help them to desire to come to Jesus. I forbid the enemy from deceiving them and pray that Your grace would be poured out upon each one of their lives. I ask You to exert Your holy influence upon their minds, wills, and emotions and to turn their hearts toward You. Thank You for promising to deliver them from the powers of darkness and bring them into the kingdom of Your Son. Nothing is impossible with You, Father, and I will let go of my concern for them by praising and thanking You for their salvation. In Jesus' name,   *Amen.*

Jehovah Rapha—the Lord Who Heals You

I am the LORD who heals you.
Exodus 15:26 NKJV

*D*o you realize what My Son, Jesus, did for you? He was beaten and crucified to pay the price for your sins. He was bruised because of your guilt and iniquities. He took your punishment in order to give you peace and prosperity. And He bore stripes on His back so that you might be healed.

Jesus purchased your freedom from the curse of sickness with His own blood. He took that curse upon himself. He was cursed with disease so that through your trust in Him, you would receive My promised blessing of health and healing.

So look to Jesus as your Healer. Rest completely in what He has provided for you. Begin to praise and worship Him as your Healer, and I will restore health to you and heal your wounds; I am the Lord who heals you from every sickness and every disease.

Scripture Reading:

Isaiah 53:5   Deuteronomy 28:15,58-61
Galatians 3:13-14   Psalm 50:23
Jeremiah 30:17

❧

Prayer:

Lord, I look to You as my Healer. Thank You for taking the curse of sickness for me so that I could receive God's promise of healing and health. You purchased my freedom from disease through Your precious blood. I praise and worship You as my Healer. I receive that healing You purchased for me. I love You, Lord, because You first loved me. In Jesus' name,   *Amen.*

Quiet Time
with the Father

*When you pray, go into your room,
and when you have shut your door,
pray to your Father who is in the
secret place; and your Father who
sees in secret will reward you openly.*
Matthew 6:6 NKJV

My child, never become so busy with life that you neglect to spend quiet time with Me. Don't be like Martha, so caught up in her chores that she made no time for Me. Instead, choose what her sister, Mary, chose, the most important thing—to set aside time to spend in My presence.

Now I understand that life can be very busy and many important activities easily occupy your time. But if you'll spend quiet time with Me, I will make all you do become more efficient by blessing the work of your hands.

So go into our secret place, shut the door, and pray. Spend time worshiping Me, reading My Word, and asking the Holy Spirit to teach and change you.

Draw close to Me, and I will draw close to you, renewing your strength like the eagle's. Look to Me with confident expectation, and I will help you walk without stumbling and run with energy and purpose. I will fill you with My joy and peace. Yes, I will bless your life for all to see if you'll only spend quiet time with Me.

Scripture Reading:

Luke 10:38-42   Deuteronomy 28:12
Isaiah 40:30-31

෴

Prayer:

Father, I want so much to spend quiet time with You. Please forgive me for allowing the "busyness" of life to take away from my time alone with You. Help me not to be distracted, but to choose the one thing I need—to sit in Your presence by worshipping You, reading and thinking upon Your Word, and praying in the secret place. Thank You for promising to reward me openly when I do so. I ask You to teach me Your ways and help me become more like You, to bring glory to You in my life. In Jesus' name,   *Amen.*

God's Plan of Redemption

For he chose us in him before the creation of the world to be holy and blameless in his sight. In love he predestined us to be adopted as his sons through Jesus Christ.
Ephesians 1:4-5

I have blessed you through My Son, Jesus, with every spiritual blessing in the heavenly realm! Long ago, even before I created the world, I loved you and chose you in Christ to be holy and without a single fault in My eyes. My unchanging plan has always been to adopt you as My child by drawing You to Me through My Son, Jesus.

I have clearly shown and proven My great love for you by the fact that while you were still a sinner, My Son, Jesus, died for you. I sent Him as an atoning sacrifice for your sins. When you received Him as your Savior and believed on His name, you became My child.

Through your trust in Him, you have redemption through His blood—the forgiveness of your sins—because of the riches of My gracious favor that I lavished upon you.

P.S. GOD LOVES YOU!

I have delivered you, saved you, and called you to live a holy life, not because of your good works, but because of My own purpose and grace, which I gave to you in Christ Jesus before the world began.

Scripture Reading:

Ephesians 1:1-7   *Romans 5:8*
1 John 2:2   *2 Timothy 1:9*

❧

Prayer:

Heavenly Father, Your love for me was so great that You were willing to sacrifice Your only Son. You had this plan for me before the beginning of time. Thank You so much for redeeming me and forgiving me of all my sins through Jesus. Because of Him, I am holy and without fault in Your eyes. I know that You have saved me, not because of my good works, but because of Your goodness and grace. Thank You for choosing me and drawing me to You. I love You, Lord, and I will serve You all the days of my life. In Jesus' name,   *Amen.*

Love One Another

*The entire law is summed up
in a single command: "Love
your neighbor as yourself."*
Galatians 5:14

*M*y child, you must fully understand that My entire law is summed up in this one single command: "Love your neighbor as yourself." Therefore, love is the fulfillment of My law.

Since I loved you so much, you also should love others. By this, all men will know you are truly My disciple. Imitate Me, as My beloved child, and live a life of love.

Therefore, clothe yourself with compassion, kindness, humility, gentleness, and patience. Forgive others of any wrong they've done to you. Forgive as I have forgiven you.

Don't envy others or become offended by something they've said or done. Get rid of all bitterness, rage, and anger; because this does not create the righteous life I desire.

I know you are not able to do this in your own strength. But look to Me and ask Me to strengthen you; I will create in you the desire and power to love others with My unfailing, unconditional love.

P.S. GOD LOVES YOU!

When you pursue righteousness and love, you will find abundant life, prosperity, and honor, for when you are faithful to love others, your life will be richly blessed.

Scripture Reading:

Philippians 2:13	*Romans 13:9-10*
Ephesians 4:26	*Proverbs 21:21*
1 John 4:12	*John 13:35*
Ephesians 5:1-2	*Colossians 3:12-13*
1 Corinthians 13:4-5	*Proverbs 28:20*

~&

Prayer:

Heavenly Father, forgive me for the times I haven't walked in love toward others. I ask You to cleanse me from all unrighteousness. I desire to become more like You. Help me love my spouse, my children, and others with Your unconditional love. Teach me to love them the way You love them. I ask You to strengthen me by Your grace to be patient, kind, and forgiving to those who have hurt me. I know that as I walk in Your love, Your abundant blessings will overtake me. But most of all, Lord, I want my life to glorify You. I want others to see You in me. In Jesus' name,   *Amen.*

God Wants You to Be Healthy

*My son, attend to my words; consent
and submit to my sayings. Let them
not depart from your sight; keep them
in the center of your heart. For they
are life to those who find them, healing
and health to all their flesh.*
Proverbs 4:20-22 AMP

My child, I want you to understand just how
much I love you. I truly desire to prosper you
in every way—including health for your body—even as
your soul prospers. Humbly receive My Word into your
mind and heart, for it has the power to prosper your soul.

So think upon My commands, My counsel, and My
promises; agree with them and humbly receive them into
your life. Don't let My words depart from your sight; keep
them in your heart, for they will bring life, health, and
healing to your whole body.

Love and worship Me with all your heart, and I will
bless your daily sustenance. I will remove sickness from
your midst. You won't miscarry or be barren in your land,

and I will give you a long, good life. I will restore you to health and heal all your wounds, for I am the Lord who heals you.

Scripture Reading:

3 John 2	Psalm 107:20
Proverbs 4:20-22	Exodus 23:25-26
Jeremiah 30:17	Exodus 15:26

Prayer:

Heavenly Father, it is wonderful to realize how much You love me. You desire that I be healthy in every way, even as my soul prospers. My soul will prosper as I think upon Your commands, counsels, and promises and humbly receive them into my life. I will keep them in the center of my heart, knowing that Your Word will bring life and health to my whole body; it is medicine to my body. Help me follow Your ways and trust in Your promises. I'm trusting You to take sickness from my midst and bless me with a long, good life. Thank You, Lord, for Your abundant goodness. In Jesus' name,   Amen.

Abide in Christ

I am like a green pine tree;
your fruitfulness comes from me.
Hosea 14:8

I am the true Vine, and you are My branch. You live because of Me. I have made you holy by cleansing you with the water of My Word.

Abide in Me, and I will abide in you. Just as no branch can bear fruit without abiding in the vine, neither can you bear fruit unless you abide and trust in Me.

As you learn to daily rely and depend on Me, your life will produce the fruits of love, joy, peace, patience, kindness, goodness, faithfulness, humility, and self-control.

I am the Vine, and you are My branch. When you trust and rely on Me, you will bear abundant fruit, but if you depend upon your own strength, you will produce nothing.

When you bear much fruit, your life honors and glorifies Me, and you show yourself to truly be My disciple.

I have loved you just as the Father has loved Me; now abide in My love. If you abide in My love and My words abide in you, you can ask Me for whatever you desire, and I will do it for you.

I have told you these things so that My joy may be in you and that your joy and gladness may be full and overflowing.

Scripture Reading:

John 15:1-5, 7-9, 11   Ephesians 5:26
Galatians 5:22-23

~&

Prayer:

Heavenly Father, I want my life to honor and glorify You. I know that as the fruit of the spirit produces in my life, I will shine with Your glory and goodness. I will abide and trust in You. I ask You to change me from glory to glory by the power of Your Spirit. I want to be more like You. I know I can't change myself. The truth is, apart from You I can do nothing. My heart overflows with joy as I think upon Your love for me. I will rejoice in You all day long. In Jesus' name,   *Amen.*

Obedience Brings Blessing

Blessed (happy and to be envied)
rather are those who hear the
Word of God and obey and practice it!
Luke 11:28 AMP

Your life will overflow with My blessings when
you hear My Word and choose to obey it.

Get rid of all uncleanness—unforgiveness, offense,
resentment, anger, doubt, jealousy, and envy—and in a
humble spirit receive My Word. Implanted in your heart,
it has the power to heal your mind and emotions.

Obey My teachings, but not in your own strength. Ask
Me to help, and I will give you the desire and power to do
what pleases Me.

Don't merely listen to My Word; *practice* it. Many of
My children have been deceived by reasoning contrary to
the truth. They follow their own ways instead of Mine.

If you listen to My Word without acting upon it, it is like
viewing your face in the mirror but, in turning away, forgetting
your own image. If you don't practice My Word upon
hearing it, you will walk away and forget what it says.

However, if you look carefully and diligently into My Word, persevering in action, you will be blessed in every area of your life. My blessings will overtake you, and your life will glorify Me.

If you abide in My Word and live according to it, you are truly My disciple. You will know the truth, and the truth will set you free.

Scripture Reading:

Luke 11:28	*James 1:21-25*
Philippians 2:12-13	*Deuteronomy 28:2*
John 15:8	*John 8:31-32*

Prayer:

Heavenly Father, create in me the desire and ability to do what pleases You. Help me listen to Your Word and obey it. I will search Your Word for Your counsel concerning my marriage, my children, and my relationships with others. I will follow Your ways, for I know this will bring Your overflowing blessings into my life. I want to have a Godly family and a life that glorifies You. Lead me to the truth, and bring victory into every area of my life. In Jesus' name,   *Amen.*

Only Believe

Don't be afraid; just believe.
Mark 5:36

*M*y child, don't allow yourself to be worried or anxious about anything; only believe and trust Me to bring to pass the promises I have given you.

My power is at work in your life when you choose to trust and believe. Then I'm able to do exceedingly, abundantly above all that you could ask for or even imagine. Remember, all things are possible if you will only believe.

Be strong and courageous. Don't be afraid or discouraged, for I am with you. I promise I won't fail you or forsake you. I am faithful—reliable, trustworthy, and true to My promises—and you can completely depend upon Me.

So let your heart rejoice in Me as you trust in My holy name. Wait for Me, and put your hope in My Word. I am the Lord your God; when you trust confidently in Me, you will never be disappointed. Begin to rejoice in all that I have promised you, for My Word will do a powerful work in your life if you will only choose to believe it.

Scripture Reading:

Mark 5:36	Mark 11:24
Ephesians 1:19	Ephesians 3:20
Mark 9:23	1 Chronicles 28:20
1 Corinthians 1:9	Psalm 33:21
Psalm 130:5	Isaiah 49:23
Psalm 119:162	1 Thessalonians 2:13

❧

Prayer:

Heavenly Father, I believe Your Word; help my unbelief. Forgive me for doubting Your promises and allowing worried and anxious thoughts to stay in my mind. I ask You to cleanse me from this unrighteousness. I realize that if I want Your power to be at work in my life, I must believe You. I rejoice in Your promises, as one who finds great riches. I choose to trust in Your Word. I have put my hope in You, and I know I will not be disappointed; because You are faithful— reliable, trustworthy, and true to Your every promise. In Jesus' name, Amen.

Financial Abundance

I am Abraham's servant. The Lord has blessed my master abundantly, and he has become wealthy. He has given him sheep and cattle, silver and gold, menservants and maidservants, and camels and donkeys.
Genesis 24:34-35

Listen to My Word, walk in My ways, and worship Me with a thankful heart. Then I will bring you to a place where your food is plentiful and nothing is lacking.

Remember to always have a thankful heart toward Me for all the blessings I have given you, for this is the time to be careful! Beware that in your plenty, you don't forget Me and begin to disobey My Word.

For when I have abundantly blessed you, your life will become full and prosperous; you will live in a fine home, and your bank accounts will be filled with plenty. This is when you must watch out. Beware that you don't become proud and say, "My great skill and wisdom have brought me this wealth."

Always remember that it is I who gives you the power to obtain wealth. I do this to establish My covenant promise.

When I have given you riches, possessions, contentment in your work, and the good health to enjoy them all, remember: this is My gift to you, for I desire to fill your life with My blessings.

Scripture Reading:
Deuteronomy 8:6-18   Ecclesiastes 5:18-20

❧

Prayer:
Heavenly Father, thank You for revealing that Your plan for me is not to live in lack, but it is to be abundantly blessed in my finances. I will never forget that it is You who gives me the power to obtain wealth. I'm so grateful for Your many blessings. Thank You for blessing me so that I can be a blessing to others. I will give abundantly to further the Gospel and help the poor in order that Your love and goodness be reflected in me. Thank You, Lord, for using me in this manner. In Jesus' name,   Amen.

God Will Reveal
His Plan for You

❧

Roll your works upon the Lord
[commit and trust them wholly to Him;
He will cause your thoughts to become
agreeable to His will, and] so shall
your plans be established and succeed.
Proverbs 16:3 AMP

Simply look to Me, and I will guide you toward My specific plan for your life. I know what your future holds. I've already laid out the plan. So commit everything you do into My hands, and trust Me completely; then I will cause your thoughts to be agreeable to My will. Your plans will become My plans, and your success will be guaranteed.

Your eyes have not seen nor your ears heard all that I have planned and prepared for you, but as you pray and fellowship with Me, I will reveal these things to you by My Spirit. I will put My plans into your mind; you will know exactly what My purpose is for your life and the paths that I want you to take.

So set yourself to seek after Me, and I will instruct you in the way you should go; as long as you earnestly seek Me with all your heart, I will cause you to prosper and succeed. I will show you the path for your life and fill you with joy in My presence.

Scripture Reading:

Psalm 32:8	Psalm 139:16
Proverbs 16:3	1 Corinthians 2:9-10,16
2 Chronicles 26:3-5	Psalm 16:11

❧

Prayer:

Heavenly Father, I ask You to reveal to me Your plans for my life. I acknowledge You and seek after Your counsel and wisdom. I ask You to make my thoughts agreeable to Your will for my life. I don't want to follow my own plans—I want to follow Yours. Thank You for revealing to me the direction in which I should go. I know that when I follow Your will for my life, my plans will be established and succeed. In Jesus' name,   *Amen.*

Train Up a Child

❧

*Train up a child in the way he
should go: and when he is old,
he will not depart from it.*
Proverbs 22:6 KJV

*T*rain your children by being a Godly example in
their lives. Put My commandments within your
own mind and heart. Then teach and impress these
commandments diligently upon the minds and hearts of
your children. Surround them with My Word! Talk about My
Word to them when you're sitting in your house, when
you're driving in your car, before they go to bed, and when
they wake up in the morning. Train your children to follow
My ways, and when they reach maturity, they will not
depart from them.

I know you face challenges in raising your children.
But if you'll ask Me for wisdom, I will show you how to
effectively handle the situations you face. Don't grow
weary in training and disciplining them, for in due season
you will reap a harvest of blessing in their lives.

It's never easy to discipline your children, but remember My promises concerning them. If you'll follow My instructions, it will bring about a peaceful fruit of righteousness in them. Yes, others will see My character reflected in them, and they will shine with My glory and bring much joy to your heart.

Scripture Reading:

Deuteronomy 6:6-7	Proverbs 22:6
James 1:5	Galatians 6:9
Hebrews 12:11	Proverbs 29:15,17

❧

Prayer:

Heavenly Father, I ask for Your grace to be a Godly parent to my children. I ask for Your wisdom in training them. I will follow Your way of discipline, for I know it will bring Your blessings upon their lives. I will put my trust in Your promise that when I train them to follow Your ways, they will not depart from You as they grow up. Because of Your faithfulness, I know that I will see Your righteousness shining bright in my children's lives. In Jesus' name,

Amen.

161

God's Promises Concerning Your Children

You can also be very sure that God will rescue the children of the godly.
Proverb 11:21 TLB

*T*his is My promise concerning your children: I will pour My Spirit upon them, blessing them abundantly! They'll prosper as trees planted near streams of living water, and they'll rise and say, "I belong to the Lord!"

The Holy Spirit won't abandon them, and they'll turn from evil and want to do good. They'll be My disciples, obedient to My will, and have great peace. This promise is for your children and your grandchildren as well.

This is My covenant promise to you: I will put the reverential fear of the Lord in the hearts of your children, so they will love and obey Me with all their hearts and souls. I will rejoice over them to do them good, filling their lives with My many blessings.

Don't worry about your children; instead trust Me. I've promised that they'll be saved—I will deliver them from the hand of the enemy.

So rejoice in My Word, and watch My powerful work in their lives; I can well do what I have promised.

Scripture Reading:

Isaiah 44:3-5	*Isaiah 59:21*
Isaiah 54:13	*Jeremiah 32:38-42*
Philippians 4:6	*Isaiah 49:25*
Acts 16:31	*Proverbs 11:21*
Jeremiah 31:16-17	*Psalm 50:23*
Romans 4:20-21	

❦

Prayer:

Heavenly Father, pour out Your Spirit upon my children and bless them abundantly. I ask You to work within them so that they obey and love You with all their hearts and souls. Your Word says they shall be Your disciples, obedient to Your will, and have great peace. I know my children will be delivered from the hand of the enemy. Your Word gives me hope for them because You cannot lie. I won't worry about them anymore; instead I will praise You and rejoice in Your promise for my family's salvation, for I know You have the power to do what You have promised. In Jesus' name,   *Amen.*

A Successful Future

He set himself to seek God in the days of Zechariah, who instructed him in the things of God; and as long as he sought (inquired of, yearned for) the Lord, God made him prosper.
2 Chronicles 26:5 AMP

*D*iligently seek after Me. Search My Word as though you were searching for hidden treasures. As long as you'll seek after Me with all your heart, I will cause you to prosper in every area of your life.

I will bless you with a future filled with hope—a future of success, not of suffering. You will turn back to me and ask for help, and I will answer your prayers. You will worship me with all your heart, and I will be with you.

Jeremiah 29:11-13 CEV

As you trust Me to help you obey My Word, I promise to make you abundantly prosperous in everything you do. I will take great delight in prospering you and leading you toward success.

Speak My Word over your life. Don't let it depart from your mouth. Think upon My promises throughout the day and even into the night, and be careful to do what My Word says. As you do this, I promise you will be a success in your marriage, as a parent, in your business, in your relationships, in your finances, and in everything you do.

Scripture Reading:

2 Chronicles 26:5   Jeremiah 29:11-13

Deuteronomy 30:8-9   Joshua 1:8

❧

Prayer:

Heavenly Father, I will diligently seek You with all my heart. I want to know You and Your ways. Help me to love others with Your love. I won't let Your Word depart from my mouth. Instead, I will speak what it says about my family, my finances, my health, and my future. I rejoice in Your promises, Lord, for You have promised me a future of success. You delight in prospering me, Lord, and that makes me realize just how much You love me. Help me to become more like You. In Jesus' name,   Amen.

God's Plan for Your Marriage

❧

But Jesus said. . . . For this reason a
man shall leave [behind] his father
and his mother and be joined to his
wife . . . And the two shall become
one flesh. . . . What therefore God
has united (joined together),
let not man separate or divide.
Mark 10:5, 7-9 AMP

*M*y will for your marriage is written in My Word.
Spouses must be subject to one another out of
reverence for Christ.

Husbands should love their wives as Christ loved the
church—nourishing, protecting, and cherishing them with
affection and sympathy, and without harshness, bitterness,
or resentfulness.

In return, I have commanded wives to respect and show
reverence for their husbands—regarding, honoring, prefer-
ring, deferring to, loving, and admiring them exceedingly.

You can be confident in this: if you ask Me to effect My
will in your marriage, I will do it!

So humbly ask Me, and I will pour My grace upon your
marriage. I will create in you both the desire and ability to

be the partners I have called you to be. I will bless your marriage, and you will overflow in love for one another when you completely trust in Me.

Scripture Reading:

Ephesians 5:21-33	*1 John 5:14-15*
Philippians 2:13	*Colossians 4:19*
2 Corinthians 12:9	*James 4:6*
1 Thessalonians 3:12	*Proverbs 3:33*
Proverbs 16:20	

❧

Prayer:

Heavenly Father, create Your will in my marriage. Forgive me for the times I have disobeyed Your Word regarding my spouse. Change me by Your grace into the partner You want me to be. Grant me the desire and ability to love my spouse with Your unconditional love. Lord, I know that as I trust You to help me love with Your unfailing love, You will bring Your will into my marriage. I humbly ask for the grace we need to change. Work in us by the power of Your Spirit and cause us to increase and overflow with love for one another. I will trust You, Lord, for I want our marriage to glorify You. In Jesus' name, Amen.

God Wants to
Bless Your Marriage

❧

Now to him who is able to do
immeasurably more than all we ask
or imagine, according to his power
that is at work within us.
Ephesians 3:20

*S*trife, anger, resentment, and unforgiveness in
your marriage are part of the curse of the law.
Jesus purchased your freedom from this curse upon your
marriage so that when you put your trust in Him, My
promised blessings of love, joy, peace, and fulfillment will
rest upon your relationship.

My grace is all you need to experience My best in your
marriage. I will create in you both the power and desire to
love one another with My unfailing love. As My power and
love flow through you, I can bring to pass My plans for
your marriage and do far more than you could ever pray,
dream, or desire.

Nothing is impossible with Me, for I can change the
heart of a king. Yes, I will heal, restore, and bless your
marriage if you will humbly and completely trust Me to
change you into the spouse I created you to be.

Scripture Reading:

Deuteronomy 28:15, 54, 56	*Galatians 3:13-14*
2 Corinthians 12:9	*James 4:5-6*
2 Corinthians 1:12 AMP	*Philippians 2:13*
Ephesians 3:20	*Luke 1:37*
Proverbs 21:1	*2 Corinthians 1:20*

❧

Prayer:

Lord, thank You for redeeming me from a curse upon my marriage. I now realize that through trusting in You, I can experience Your promised blessings upon my marriage relationship. I realize I can't do Your will without Your grace working in my life. I humbly ask You to change me into the spouse You called me to be. I know that as Your power works in me, You can do abundantly more in my marriage than I could ever pray, dream, or desire.

I ask for Your grace to be at work in my spouse also. Please create in us the desire and ability to love one another with Your unconditional love. As we partake of Your promises of love, joy, and peace in our marriage, our lives will truly glorify You. In Jesus name, Amen.

God's Healing Power

~

*Worship the LORD your God, and his
blessing will be on your food and
water. I will take away sickness
from among you, and none will
miscarry or be barren in your land.
I will give you a full life span.*
Exodus 23:25-26

*W*orship Me as your Healer, and My healing
virtue will flow through you. I will bless your
sustenance. I will take away sickness from among you and
give you a long life upon the earth.

If you are sick, call for those who are spiritually
mature in the church to pray over you and anoint you with
oil in the name of My Son, Jesus. The prayer that is offered
to Me in faith will make My healing power available, and I
will restore health to your body.

I will use you to bring My healing power to others. My
Word says in Mark 16:15-18 KJV,

*Go ye into all the world, and preach the gospel to
every creature. He that believeth and is baptized
shall be saved. . . . And these signs shall follow them
that believe; In my name shall they cast out devils;*

they shall speak with new tongues . . . they shall lay hands on the sick, and they shall recover.

So believe My Word, and as you minister the good news of the Gospel, I will cause all these signs to follow you wherever you go.

Scripture Reading:

Exodus 23:25-26   James 5:14-16

Mark 16:15-18

❧

Prayer:

Heavenly Father, I worship You as My Healer, and I ask that Your healing virtue flow through every cell of my body. I want to be strong and healthy in order to bring the good news of the Gospel to others who are sick and hurting. I choose to believe Your Word and Your promise that I shall lay my hands on the sick in the name of Jesus, and they shall recover. Thank you, Lord, for watching over Your Word and performing it in my life. In Jesus' name,   *Amen.*

Trust God
Rather than Man

~&~

It is *better to trust in the* LORD
than to put confidence in man.
Psalm 118:8 KJV

*M*y child, don't put your hope in any man.
Instead, put your hope in Me. You will miss
out on My plan of prosperity and peace if you choose to
put your trust in man. If you put your hope in man instead
of Me, you will be like a withered tree in the desert with no
hope for your future. You will dwell in parched places in
the wilderness, never seeing the promises I have for you
come to pass.

Yet if you put your confidence in Me, My promised
blessings will reside in every area of your life. You will be
like a tree planted by streams of living water; you won't
worry or fear when your faith is tested, but you will rejoice
in the promises I have given you. You won't be anxious in
trials, nor will you cease bearing fruit.

Yes, if you keep your mind and heart on Me, trusting in My promises, you will grow in grace and be rich in the virtues of trust, love, and contentment. You will be a living testimony of proof that My Word is true, and I am faithful to all My promises.

Scripture Reading:

Psalm 118:8   Jeremiah 17:5-8

Psalm 92:12-15

❧

Prayer:

Heavenly Father, forgive me for turning from You and putting my hope in man. When I look to others or myself, I sometimes become discouraged, but when I look to and trust only You, I realize no man can keep Your promises from coming to pass in my life. I choose this day to keep my mind on You and trust You with all of my heart. You have promised wonderful things for my family and me, so I won't fear when my faith is tested. I will rejoice in Your promises and the victory I have in You. I want my life to be a living testimony of Your faithfulness to all Your promises. In Jesus' name,   *Amen.*

Destined to Be like Jesus

❧

For those whom He foreknew [of whom He was aware and loved beforehand], He also destined from the beginning [foreordaining them] to be molded into the image of His Son [and share inwardly His likeness].
Romans 8:29 AMP

*B*efore you were even conceived, I knew you. From the beginning of time you were a part of My plan, and I loved you with all of My heart. It was then that I destined you to be molded into the image of My Son, Jesus.

I am your Heavenly Father. You are the clay, and I am the Potter; you are the work of My hands.

You are My own workmanship. I created you in Christ Jesus to do good works, which I have prepared in advance for you to do.

As you daily trust in Jesus, My Spirit of grace will be at work in you, and where My Spirit is at work, there is freedom from all sin and deliverance from bondage.

As you continue to look to Jesus and behold His glory, you are being transformed by the power of My Spirit from glory to glory into His very own image.

You can be confident of this very thing: I have begun a good work in you, and I will continue to develop that good work, perfecting it and bringing it to full completion in you.

Scripture Reading:

Romans 8:30

Ephesians 2:10

Philippians 1:6

Isaiah 64:8

2 Corinthians 3:16-18

❧

Prayer:

Heavenly Father, Your plan for my life is to mold and change me into the image of Jesus. I realize that I can't become like Him by trying hard enough, for in my own power and ability, I can do nothing. Forgive me for not trusting You to do the work in me. I ask You, Lord, to work in me by the power of Your Spirit and change me into Your image. Help me to love others with Your love so that my life will glorify You. In Jesus name,   Amen.

Bear One Another's Burdens

~

*Brethren, if a man be overtaken in a
fault, ye which are spiritual, restore
such an one in the spirit of meekness;
considering thyself, lest thou also
be tempted. Bear ye one another's
burdens, and so fulfil the law of Christ.*
Galatians 6:1-2 KJV

If you see other believers overtaken by sin in their
lives, don't judge or condemn them. Don't look
down on them, lest you also be tempted.

Bear their burdens and troublesome faults by praying
for their deliverance. When you do this, you are perfectly
fulfilling the law of Christ—the law of love.

Trust completely in My promises concerning them
because I have promised that if you will pray for them, I
will give them life. Yes, I will deliver them from the snare of
the enemy. I will exert My holy influence upon their minds,
wills, and emotions and turn their hearts toward Me. I will
strengthen them and cause them to increase in Christian
character, for My grace is sufficient for their every weakness.

Your prayers will be powerful and effective, for I have
promised to deliver the ones for whom you pray. So don't

grow weary in praying for them, no matter how the situation may appear, for surely you will see them walking in victory and reflecting My glory in their life.

Scripture Reading:

Galatians 6:1-2,9	1 John 5:16
2 Corinthians 1:12 AMP	James 5:16
Job 22:30	

❧

Prayer:

Heavenly Father, I pray for _____ today, and I ask that You would give them life. I ask You to pour Your mercy and grace into their lives. Influence their minds, wills, and emotions, and turn their hearts toward You. Heal and restore them, Lord, and deliver them from all the strongholds in their lives. Open their eyes to the truth. I am determined not to become discouraged by what I see. Instead, I will continue to praise and thank You for the powerful work You are accomplishing in them. You are so faithful, and You alone can bring victory into their lives. In Jesus' name,   *Amen.*

The Word of God

*For the Word that God speaks is alive
and full of power [making it active,
operative, energizing, and effective].*
Hebrews 4:12 AMP

I sent My Word to heal you and to deliver you from destruction. Abide in My Word; hold fast to my teachings; then you will know the truth, and the truth will set you free.

Look into My Word, for it is filled with My promises, commands, and counsel to strengthen you and give you your rightful inheritance—an abundantly blessed life.

So get rid of bitterness, unforgiveness, offense, and anger. Humbly receive and welcome My Word which, implanted and rooted in your heart, contains the power to heal your mind and emotions. As you think upon My Word, it will revive you and give you life.

Let My Word have its home in your heart and dwell in you richly as you sings songs of praise.

Realize that the Scriptures are not the words of mere men, but My Word that I have spoken. My Word is alive and full of power. It will exercise superhuman power in your life when you choose to believe it.

Scripture Reading:

Psalm 107:20   John 8:31-32

Acts 20:32   James 1:21

Colossians 3:16   Hebrews 4:13

1 Thessalonians 2:13

⌒❧

Prayer:

Heavenly Father, thank You for sending Your Word to heal, deliver, and set me free. Your Word is alive and full of power. It's not merely men's words, but actually Your words spoken to me. I will dispose of all unforgiveness, offense, and anger of any kind. Your Word contains the power to heal my mind and emotions. Therefore, I will receive it into my heart. As I keep my mind on You and what You have spoken, I will know the truth, and the truth will set me free from all bondages in my life. I will let Your Word dwell richly in me as I live a life of praise and thanksgiving. I know Your Word holds the key to my inheritance in you—an abundant, blessed, and happy life. In Jesus' name,   *Amen.*

179

Deliverance from Strongholds

*(For the weapons of our warfare
are not carnal, but mighty through God
to the pulling down of strong holds:)
Casting down imaginations, and
every high thing that exalteth itself
against the knowledge of God,
and bringing into captivity every
thought to the obedience of Christ.*
2 Corinthians 10:4-5 KJV

My child, how my heart longs for you to prosper in every area of your life and for your body to be strong and healthy, yet this will only happen as your mind prospers.

Strongholds in your life keep you from stepping into the fullness of my blessings—strongholds that begin in your mind by what you choose to think upon. You will be delivered and set free from every bondage and stronghold in your life by renewing your mind to the truth of My Word.

So cast down every thought of fear, doubt, worry, skepticism, and every imagination of failure and hopelessness. Replace them with the truth of My Word by filling your mind with My promises.

I will keep you in perfect peace when you keep your mind on Me because that's when you are truly trusting Me.

So trust in Jesus with all of your heart by keeping your mind on Him because if His words abide in you, you will know the truth, and the truth will set you free. Yes, the one whom the Son sets free is free indeed!

Scripture Reading:

3 John 2   2 Corinthians 10:4-5
Isaiah 26:3   John 8:31-32,36

❧

Prayer:

Heavenly Father, thank You for revealing to me how I can be freed from strongholds in my life—things in my past that have kept me in bondage. I now realize that true freedom and victory come through renewing my mind to the truth of Your Word. I will cast down all thoughts of fear, anger, resentment, discouragement, and doubt and replace them with the truth of Your Word. I will keep my mind on You, Lord, for only through trusting in You will I experience true victory. In Jesus' name,   Amen.

Renew Your Mind

*And be not conformed to this world:
but be ye transformed by the renewing
of your mind, that ye may prove
what is that good, and acceptable,
and perfect, will of God.*
Romans 12:2 KJV

*M*y child, don't act as the world does. Instead,
be transformed into the image of Jesus by
renewing your mind on My Word. Then you will truly
come to know what My good, acceptable, and perfect will
is for you.

Lay aside the characteristics of your old nature—
arguing, lying, anger, unforgiveness, resentment, and harsh
words. Instead constantly renew your mind by keeping it
set on Me and the truth of My Word. In so doing, you are
putting on your new nature, which was created to be like
Me—righteous and holy.

If you keep your mind on those things that please the
sinful nature, the result will be misery and defeat. Choose
rather to keep your mind on those things which please Me,

and you'll experience a life filled with peace and joy and
blessings that overflow.

Scripture Reading:

Romans 12:2   *Ephesians 4:22-32*

Romans 8:4-6

❧

Prayer:

*Heavenly Father, I realize now that it is through renewing
my mind on Your Word that I am changed into Your image.
I choose to lay aside my old, unrenewed self and be
transformed by the power of Your Spirit as I keep my
mind on You and Your wonderful Word. I want my life to
bring glory to You by demonstrating Your peace, joy, and
love overflowing to others. In Jesus' name,   Amen.*

Put On the Armor of God

❧

*Put on all of God's armor so that
you will be able to stand safe against
all strategies and tricks of Satan.*
Ephesians 6:11 TLB

*D*raw your strength from Me. Remember that your struggle is, not against people, but against the powers of darkness and evil, so use My armor to resist the attack. Then when the battle is finished, you'll be waving the flag of victory.

Surround yourself with the belt of truth, which is found in My Word. Search My Word for My truth to keep the enemy from deceiving you.

Put on the breastplate of righteousness, and guard your heart with all diligence. Remember that unforgiveness, resentment, offense, and anger can bring destruction into your life.

Wear the shoes of the Gospel of peace. Be ready to share My Word with others. As you do, your spirit will be strengthened by the Good News.

Above all, add faith to the promises of My Word. When you do this, you will stop every fiery dart the enemy expels against you.

Put on the helmet of salvation by keeping your mind on Me and the many promises I have given you. Cast down every thought that is not in agreement with the truth of My Word.

Use the sword of the Spirit—the spoken Word of God. Jesus defeated Satan by saying, "It is written. . . ." In this same way, you, too, will be victorious.

Last of all, continue to pray in the Spirit. When you put on My whole armor and stand steadfast on My Word, you will experience victory in every situation.

Scripture Reading:

Ephesians 6:10-18   Psalm 119:160
Hosea 4:6   Proverbs 4:23
Ephesians 4:26-27   2 Corinthians 10:5
Matthew 4:1-11

~&

Prayer:
Heavenly Father, strengthen me by the power of Your Spirit. I will put on every piece of Your armor so that I can stand successfully against every attack of the devil. Thank you for giving me everything I need to walk in victory in every situation. The devil is the loser, and I am the winner because of Jesus. In Jesus name,   Amen.

When You Lose Someone You Love

Now also we would not have you ignorant, brethren, about those who fall asleep [in death], that you may not grieve [for them] as the rest do who have no hope [beyond the grave].
1 Thessalonians 4:13 AMP

*M*y child, I know how your heart hurts when you lose someone you love, but allow the truth of my Word to bring healing to your heart.

I don't want you to grieve as those in the world do, who have no hope beyond the grave.

I have your loved ones with me in heaven. They are walking on streets of gold, living in beautiful mansions, and swimming in the river of life. They are laughing, playing, loving, and living vivaciously.

When they came to heaven, they entered into health, peace, love, prosperity, and everlasting joy. Death has been swallowed up in complete victory. There is no defeat in death.

Rejoice for them, for they have not lost—they have gained. To be in heaven with Jesus is far better than to be on this earth.

Be encouraged by the truth that you will only miss them for a short time. Then you will see them again and never be separated from them for all eternity.

Scripture Reading:

Psalm 147:3	1 Thessalonians 4:13-18
Revelations 21:21	John 14:2
Revelations 22:1	Isaiah 57:1-2
1 Corinthians 15:54-57	Philippians 1:21,23

Prayer:

Heavenly Father, I ask You to heal my hurting heart and fill me with Your joy. I know Your grace is sufficient for me. I do miss _____, but I realize that we will see each other again. I know _____ is alive in heaven with You—happy, healthy, and whole in every way. Your Word says that we have the victory even in death. We win because of Jesus. I love You, Lord, and I thank You for preparing such a wonderful place for us to spend eternity together, forever with You. In Jesus' name,   Amen.

References

Unless otherwise indicated, all Scripture quotations are taken from the *Holy Bible, New International Version*®. NIV®. Copyright © 1973, 1978, 1984 by International Bible Society. Used by permission of Zondervan Publishing House. All rights reserved.

Scripture quotations marked AMP are taken from *The Amplified Bible. Old Testament* copyright © 1965, 1987 by Zondervan Corporation, Grand Rapids, Michigan. *New Testament* copyright © 1958, 1987 by The Lockman Foundation, La Habra, California. Used by permission.

Scripture quotations marked KJV are taken from the *King James Version* of the Bible.

Verses marked TLB are taken from *The Living Bible* © 1971. Used by permission of Tyndale House Publishers, Inc., Wheaton, Illinois 60189. All rights reserved.

Scripture quotations marked NKJV are taken from *The New King James Version*. Copyright © 1979, 1980, 1982, 1994 by Thomas Nelson, Inc.

Scripture quotations marked NLT are taken from the *Holy Bible, New Living Translation*, copyright © 1996. Used by permission of Tyndale House Publishers, Inc., Wheaton, Illinois 60189. All rights reserved.

Scripture quotations marked NAS are taken from the *New American Standard Bible*. Copyright © The Lockman Foundation 1960, 1962, 1963, 1968, 1971, 1972, 1973, 1975, 1977, 1995. Used by permission.

Scripture quotations marked CEV are from the *Contemporary English Version*, copyright © 1991, 1992, 1995 by the American Bible Society. Used by permission.

About the Author

Connie Witter has taught ladies' Bible studies for seven years. She teaches women how to live a victorious Christian life through daily trusting and relying upon Jesus and the promises we have in Him.

She is the author of two other Honor books: *P.S. God Loves You!* and *P.S. God Loves You Too!* She has also written a Bible study, *God's Great and Precious Promises.*

Connie is married to a wonderful husband, Tony, and is the mother of four beautiful children, Justin, Jared, Kristen, and Victoria. They make their home in Broken Arrow, Oklahoma.

If you would like to write the author,
you may contact her at:
Connie Witter
P.O. Box 3064
Broken Arrow, OK 74013-3064

Additional copies of this book
are available from your local bookstore.

Also by Connie Witter:
P.S. God Loves You!
P.S. God Loves You Too!

If you have enjoyed this book, or if it has
impacted your life, we would like to hear from you.

Please contact us at:
Honor Books
Department E
P.O. Box 55388
Tulsa, Oklahoma 74155
Or by e-mail at info@honorbooks.com

Honor Books
Tulsa, Oklahoma